2015

Love to Bryan + Kimbrooke

Blessings from

Chad + Hillary

the **BEST YEAR**
of your marriage

the
BEST YEAR
of your marriage

52 DEVOTIONS TO BRING
YOU CLOSER

JIM & JEAN DALY

– GENERAL EDITORS –

WITH PAUL BATURA

TYNDALE HOUSE PUBLISHERS, INC.

CAROL STREAM, ILLINOIS

The Best Year of Your Marriage: 52 Devotions to Bring You Closer

Copyright © 2014 Focus on the Family

A Focus on the Family book published by Tyndale House Publishers, Inc., Carol Stream, Illinois 60188

Focus on the Family and the accompanying logo and design are federally registered trademarks of Focus on the Family, Colorado Springs, CO 80995.

TYNDALE, Tyndale's quill logo, and *LeatherLike* are registered trademarks of Tyndale House Publishers, Inc.

All Scripture quotations, unless otherwise indicated, are taken from the *Holy Bible, New International Version®*. NIV®. Copyright © 1973, 1978, 1984 by International Bible Society. Used by permission of Zondervan Publishing House. All rights reserved. Scripture quotations marked (AMP) are taken from *The Amplified Bible*, Copyright © 1954, 1958, 1962, 1964, 1965, 1987 by The Lockman Foundation. All rights reserved. Used by permission. (www.Lockman.org)

Portions of this book are adapted from *Complete Guide to the First Five Years of Marriage*, ISBN-10: 1-58997-041-1; ISBN-13: 978-1-58997-041-0. Copyright © 2006 by Focus on the Family.

Some names and details of certain case studies in this book have been changed to protect the privacy of the individuals involved. The events and underlying principles, however, have been conveyed as accurately as possible.

No part of this publication may be reproduced, stored in a retrieval system, or transmitted in any form or by any means—electronic, mechanical, photocopy, recording, or otherwise—without prior permission of Focus on the Family.

Cover design by Jennifer Ghionzoli
Cover photograph of couple holding hands copyright © mediaphotos/Getty Images. All rights reserved. Bird artwork copyright © debra hughes/Shutterstock. All rights reserved.

Library of Congress Cataloging-in-Publication Data pending
ISBN 978-1-62405-136-4
Printed in China

1 2 3 4 5 6 7 8 9 / 19 18 17 16 15 14

CONTENTS

THE AUTHORS

Lon Adams, M.A., L.M.F.T.
Paul Batura
Jim and Jean Daly
Sheryl DeWitt, L.M.F.T., L.M.F.C.C.
James Groesbeck, L.C.S.W., L.M.F.T.
Daniel Huerta, M.S.W., L.C.S.W.
Romie Hurley, L.P.C., N.C.C.
Rob Jackson, M.S., L.P.C., L.M.H.C., N.C.C.
Betty Jordan, R.N., M.A., L.P.C.
Sam Kennedy, M.A., L.M.F.T.
Sandra Lundberg, Psy.D.
Glenn Lutjens, M.A., L.M.F.T.
Randy Southern
Amy Swierczek
Phillip J. Swihart, Ph.D.
Mitch Temple, M.S., L.M.F.T.
James Vigorito, Ph.D.
Wilford Wooten, M.S.W., L.M.F.T., L.C.S.W.

ACKNOWLEDGMENTS

We appreciate the monumental editing needed for a volume encompassing the work of so many diverse authors, which was provided by John Duckworth, senior book producer, Focus on the Family. We also wish to recognize our colleague, Aarin Hovanec, for her perceptive observations and comments. In addition, we're thankful for Sharon Manney's technical assistance in the preparation of this manuscript.

> —*Phillip J. Swihart, Ph.D. and Wilford Wooten, M.S.W., L.M.F.T., L.C.S.W.*

FOREWORD

By Jim and Jean Daly

Remember the moment you first fell in love?

It seems like an easy, straightforward question. But is it?

Many of us, when asked, find our minds wandering back to our first "crush" or an innocent kiss stolen under the stars. At the time we thought we were "in love," but if we were really young, chances are we weren't.

Instead, we were in love with the idea of it all, not the person whose hand we first held.

There's a big difference—as the two of us know.

We're still passionate about marriage—helping couples experience marriages that don't just survive but thrive. Having recently passed our twenty-seventh anniversary, we can honestly say our marriage is getting better by the year.

But we haven't always experienced this upward trajectory. There have been tough times, as there always are. There have been seasons of struggle and periods of frustration. We'll share some of them in the following pages. Through it all, though, we've challenged ourselves to keep close by seeking to remain in consistent fellowship with the Lord.

We don't know where you are on the marital spectrum, of course. Maybe you're newly married and the future looks as bright as the morning sun. Maybe you find yourself in the "doldrums," a period of stagnation; things aren't really bad, but they aren't very good, either. Or maybe you're doing pretty well and want to maintain that status—which is why you're reading this book.

Wherever you are on the marriage continuum, there's something here for you. Because marriage was God's idea, He wants the very best for our relationships. It must break His heart to see so much strain, strife, and stress battering homes around the world.

It need not be this way.

Designed as a gift to mankind that brings glory to the Creator, marriage is an institution critical to the sustainability and stability of society. God has built into every human being a desire for companionship and craving to love and be loved.

There are some who seem determined to undermine the importance of marriage as God intended. Sadly, these individuals and movements grab the headlines. But they don't represent the majority opinion. David Popenoe, a former professor of sociology at Rutgers University, recently suggested that people who say traditional marriage is becoming obsolete might be voicing a fear, not expressing a wish. We think that's pretty insightful.

If you ask people what they fear most, it's not uncommon to hear talk of terrorism, death, pain, and even public speaking and spiders. Yet, if you speak more intimately with these same people—or even watch how they live as opposed to listening to what they say—you often get a very different take on what truly burdens them.

Since God created people for companionship, it makes sense that many of us fear loneliness most of all. Studies have confirmed that loneliness is on the rise in the U.S., a curious thing since we're increasingly connected—at least technologically speaking.

By some estimates, 60 million Americans (20 percent) are lonely. A significant percentage of these people have absolutely nobody with whom to talk over important or intimate matters.

It's no wonder that many would fear the loss of marriage as an institution, especially given its emotional, spiritual, and physical benefits. If there's no marriage, there's no hope of that long walk into the sunset with your aging spouse by your side.

We're reminded of a favorite observation from the late President Ronald Reagan, whose love affair with his beloved Nancy has been so well chronicled. Regarding the gift and beauty of marriage, consider the Gipper's poignant reflection in a 1989 interview with reporter Mike Wallace:

> Nancy's power was the power of, well, giving me a
> marriage that was like an adolescent's dream of what
> marriage should be. Clark Gable had some words once,
> when he said there is nothing more wonderful for a man

than to know as he approaches his own doorstep that
someone on the other side of that door is listening for
the sound of his footsteps.[1]

Even while he was president, Mr. Reagan used to stand by
the window in the White House and watch for the lights of the
car that would bring his Nancy home.

We're called not only to preserve the God-ordained institution of marriage and highlight its benefits and His reasons for it;
we're to model it well, too. Perhaps many people fear the loss of
marriage because they've never seen a healthy one in their own
families or communities. We'd be wise to quell that anxiety by
living out our marriages as they were intended to be.

We hope this book helps you do that. We're delighted to
add our perspective to it. In fact, we consider it a privilege to
contribute. Most of what you're about to read has been lov-
ingly and prayerfully written by the counselors of Focus on the
Family. How we admire these wise women and men who day
in and day out help millions of people see their relationships as
God sees them. May the Lord bless them—and you and your
spouse—as you journey through these pages.

INTRODUCTION

By Phillip J. Swihart, Ph.D. and
Wilford Wooten, M.S.W., L.M.F.T., L.C.S.W.

Most marriages start with the delight of "being in love." The question is what happens next. Does bliss lead to adjustment, compromises, and learning to really love another person who may have very different needs and expectations? Or does it give way to poorly handled conflict, power struggles, and deepening frustration and resentment?

Even in marriages that end up thriving, marital bliss is often replaced by marital stress. Financial problems, for instance, challenge many couples. So do schedules; if some spouses feel as if they never see each other, it's because they never do.

Trying to agree on priorities is stressful, too. What purchases should you make? What should you forgo? Where should you live? Just finding out what your spouse thinks is normal to spend on clothes can be enlightening—in a very negative way.

Other stressors include getting used to in-laws. Discovering what your mate's family is really like can be a shock.

So is finding that neither of you seems to have any conflict management skills. As one comedian noted, "My wife and I never fight; we just have moments of intense fellowship." Instead of dealing constructively with the inevitable conflicts and disagreements found in any marriage, you may quickly devolve into blaming, yelling, and withdrawing—a toxic cocktail that can send a marriage spiraling downward.

And then there's sex. Whatever happened to the glorious expectations you had in that wonder-world of dating? It may only take a few months of marital reality for the fantasies of "true love" and sexual excitement to clash with the disappointments of sharing a bed with another imperfect person who's sometimes tough to like, let alone love.

Another stressor for many married couples is pregnancy—and the joys and strains of parenting. Trying to learn a whole new skill set is hard enough, but it's much harder when you're desperate for a few more hours of sleep. Even spouses with more than the usual maturity find themselves unusually irritable and hard to get along with.

The spiritual dimension of your relationship can be a point of contention, too. This often forms fertile ground for spiritual attack by an enemy who would love to destroy a relationship that God has blessed as holy.

Many of these challenges stem from distorted expectations. More and more, we want everything to happen on demand. But marriage doesn't work that way.

The apostle Paul advised Christians to "work out your salvation with fear and trembling" (Philippians 2:12). As radio Bible teacher Alistair Begg has noted, we need to do the same in our marriages.

This is a book about working things out—trembling or

otherwise. But it doesn't just dispense advice. It gives you and your spouse a way to spend special time together, talking about things that matter, considering God's Word, praying, and taking action to strengthen and recharge your relationship. You can share these times as often as you like; once a week is a good place to start. It's our hope and prayer that these devotions will be a rich source of help and encouragement on your journey through the partnership called marriage.

There's another distinctive to this volume, too. Most of the authors are current or former professional staff members with Focus on the Family's counseling department. They're committed Christians and highly qualified mental health, marriage, and family therapists with many years of combined experience in working with thousands of couples like you.

Marriage is an adventure. As you enjoy your God-given partnership, enjoy this book, too.

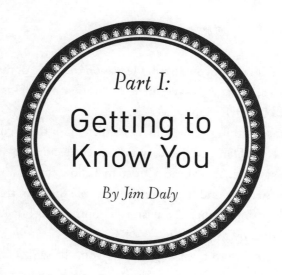

Part I:

Getting to Know You

By Jim Daly

I'd like to tell you how Jean and I first met.

We first crossed paths in 1985 at a wedding in California. People often say that weddings are great places to meet people (for good reason), but at the time I wasn't interested in finding a girlfriend. Honest! I'd recently returned from a semester in Japan and graduated from college. Business degree in hand, I landed a good position with a local paper company and began the corporate climb.

I'd decided to take a break from dating. It was just something the Lord had laid on my heart. As a result of that decision, my head was clearing and my prayer life was improving. It felt great to devote my full attention to my spiritual development, not the pursuit of a pretty girl.

My good friend Dan was incredulous. We bantered about it; he respected my decision to steer clear of romance, but I could tell he was unconvinced. He was on the verge of marrying his fiancée, Tina, and asked me to be his best man. Honored, I accepted his invitation.

But something extraordinary happened on the Wednesday night before Dan and Tina's wedding. I'd decided to attend a service at Lake Arrowhead Christian Fellowship. I was not a regular attendee, and knew very few people there. In the midst of the worship service the pastor—whom I did not know—walked directly toward me.

"I have a word from the Lord for you," he said. "The Lord has picked out a wife for you. She will have a heart for the things of God." He paused and then continued. "And in the years to come you will spread the gospel of Jesus Christ to people all around the world."

I was stunned. But my heart was tender and receptive to what this man said.

That coming Saturday, at the wedding, I met Tina's good friend. Her name was Jean. Despite the fact that it was Dan and Tina's big day, they worked like crazy to get us together—and succeeded. Jean and I made some pleasant small talk, but quickly parted ways. When I returned to my table, I couldn't believe what I heard myself say to my friend Victor: "I think I met the woman I'm going to marry."

But life got busy; Jean and I didn't talk to or see one another for the next nine months! Once again our friends tried to play Cupid and orchestrated another meeting. For our first get-together (not our official first date), I escorted Jean to an Amy Grant concert at the Pacific Amphitheatre in Newport Beach. I packed a picnic dinner of grapes, cheese, crackers, and iced tea. (I later learned that Jean hated iced tea—but that night she drank it with a smile.) In the fading twilight of that warm evening, I think we both realized something good was happening. But we kept our thoughts to ourselves.

Jean was still in college and due back to classes in September for her next year at the University of California at Davis. I hated to see her go, and wasn't crazy about having a long-distance relationship.

So what does a love-struck young man in this situation do? I quit my job and moved in with my brother Mike, who happened to live in Sacramento about 40 miles from Jean's school. For two semesters I burned through savings and income from a few odd jobs while Jean worked on her pre-vet degree.

Our dating life was lots of fun. We talked and talked and talked! While Jean was still in school, I bought a ring and proposed (with her father's permission) under the shade of a large Santa Barbara oak tree.

She said "yes"!

There's more to the story, but we'll save it for later. For now, I'll just point out what strikes me when I think back to the way Jean and I met. I'm reminded that though man has his plans, God will always have His way!

I'll also encourage you to explore the readings in this

"Getting to Know You" section. As Jean and I have found, discovering each other doesn't end with the proposal or the walk down the aisle. It's a lifelong process. As you read, have fun remembering the story of how you met—and looking forward to knowing each other better with each passing week.

I

Making Time to Talk

"You who dwell in the gardens with friends in attendance, let me hear your voice! Come away, my lover, and be like a gazelle or like a young stag on the spice-laden mountains."
SONG OF SONGS 8:13-14

Caleb and Trina, recently married, didn't have much spare time. They had full-time jobs and took evening classes. They also found themselves over-invested in church duties and under-invested in each other. They spent little time together, and found even less time to converse. When they did talk, it was mostly to argue and criticize each other. They even questioned whether or not they should be married because they were "falling out of love."

One day, Caleb took a drive in the country. Long into the evening, about two miles from home, the car suddenly stopped. It had run out of gas.

Something came to Caleb's mind at that moment: His marriage was running out of fuel, too. He knew that he and his wife needed help, and needed it immediately.

Fortunately, they were referred to a marriage counselor. The first thing they learned there was the "24-5 Principle"—based in part on Deuteronomy 24:5: "If a man has recently married, he must not be sent to war or have any other duty laid on him. For one year he is to be free to stay at home and bring happiness to the wife he has married."

Like Caleb and Trina, many couples don't take enough time to talk, bond, and firmly connect with each other. How about you?

If you're a newlywed, you can apply the 24-5 Principle by making an agreement for one year. Refrain from extra responsibilities in order to focus on and establish your marriage. Bond with your spouse. Bring happiness to one another. If your church asks you to take on a major task during this time, you might say something like, "Thank you for thinking of us. We're so pleased with the church and so encouraged by all of you. But we've been strongly advised to invest in each other this first year. Please ask us again in a year or so."

What if you're past the one-year mark? You can apply the 24-5 Principle anytime by doing five things:

1. *Keep your promise to "become one."* One of the best ways to do this is by spending time talking, setting goals, going shopping, playing tennis—even reading a devotional book.

2. *Be intentional and selective.* Everyone has the same amount of time—24 hours a day. If talking really is a priority for you, you'll say no to time-stealers like TV sitcoms, reality shows, and the Internet.

3. *Be creative and perseverant.* Talk about a variety of subjects—solving problems, overcoming challenges, strengthening your spiritual life, and just having fun. And remember that bonding and connecting don't happen overnight.

4. *Enjoy and encourage uniqueness.* Think of how boring it would be to be married to yourself! Those conversations wouldn't be very interesting, would they? As you spend time together, resist the temptation to try remaking your spouse in your image. Let the Holy Spirit transform both of you into the image of Christ.

5. *Respect God's gift.* God has given you and your spouse each other. How are you nurturing that gift? Taking time to talk is part of that.

—*James Groesbeck with Amy Swierczek*

WORTH THINKING ABOUT

Read Song of Songs 8:13-14 again. What does it mean to you to hear your spouse's voice? Where are your favorite places to "come away" and talk?

WORTH PRAYING ABOUT

Ask God to help you make wise choices about how you use your time this week, and to give you wisdom to make the most of your time together.

WORTH DOING

Choose a chore or recreational activity (washing dishes, hiking, weeding the garden, etc.) that you and your spouse can do together during the next 24 hours. Make sure it's something you can do while talking. Then pick a topic you'll discuss—something positive, like planning a vacation or remembering the two best movies you ever watched together. Some conversations require lots of concentration and eye contact, but talking while doing something else can be an efficient, nonthreatening way to break the ice—especially if you haven't communicated in a while.

2

Honesty: the Best Policy?

*"Instead, speaking the truth in love, we will in all things
grow up into him who is the Head, that is, Christ."*

EPHESIANS 4:15

If you're a Christian, are you required to be "absolutely" honest
with your spouse? After all, the Scriptures are clear that lying is a
serious affront to God. Christians are to strive for honesty—and
truth is absolute, not relative.

But what does that mean when your wife asks, "Does this
dress make me look fat?" What does it mean when your husband was intimate with a girlfriend before he met you?

Being honest in the sense of telling the truth is not the same
as imparting every thought and feeling you have. Joe and Suzie
learned that the hard way.

They'd been married two years. Suzie often remembered
that Joe had been "honest" in telling her during a premarital counseling session that he'd been intimate with two other
women before becoming a Christian five years ago. As time
went by, she found herself thinking more and more about these
"other women." She decided to be "honest" and tell her husband

that if he would just answer a couple of questions, she'd be able to forget the whole thing.

Joe reluctantly agreed to talk briefly about these old girl-friends. Much to his disappointment, these "honest" answers did nothing to satisfy Suzie's increasing obsession with his history. She began to demand detailed information. Joe withdrew from Suzie's "interrogations" and refused to talk about anything in his past. This effort to be "honest" turned into a painful, ugly series of interchanges that became toxic for their relationship.

So is honesty the best policy?

Couples should be honest before making a lifelong commitment to marriage, disclosing information that could influence that decision. This includes medical and financial status, past marriages and children if any, spiritual journey and current walk in the faith, criminal history, and other "risk" factors.

In considering how honest to be in a marriage, though, it's important to examine the intent of the heart.

"Honesty" sounds pious, but can be a selfish excuse for meeting your own needs. In Suzie's case, one of her motives was trying to relieve her insecurities. She was thinking, *How do I compare? If I don't measure up, he'll be tempted again by another woman.*

Some people give their spouses too much information about past and present sinful actions and thoughts. To feel better about themselves, they dump their guilt feelings on their mates—unnecessarily hurting them. Others even offer "honest" information to create anxiety or jealousy in the spouse.

Choosing not to disclose all events of the day or all thoughts that cross your mind isn't necessarily dishonest. In fact, sometimes the loving thing to do is to keep your mouth shut.

Giving a diplomatic answer in love rather than a cold, blunt "truth" is not the same as lying. For instance, it's not particularly virtuous to "honestly" tell your husband that he's boring or not much of a lover.

And if your wife *does* ask, "Does this dress make me look fat?" the biblical admonition about "speaking the truth in love" comes to mind. The flat truth is that the dress doesn't *make* her look fat. A more diplomatic and loving response than a simple "yes" is much advised. For example, you could tell her that although you think her blue dress looks better on her, she's very attractive no matter what dress she's wearing. "No, that dress doesn't make you look fat," you might say. "You look beautiful."

Being truthful in marriage is vital. But before demanding or disclosing "all," be honest with yourself about your motives. Is this for the benefit of your partner and the relationship? Or is it really an attempt to meet some of your own needs?

—*Phillip J. Swihart*

WORTH THINKING ABOUT

Read Ephesians 4:15 again. Which seems to have a higher priority in your conversations as a couple—truth or love? What would have to change to give both "top billing"?

WORTH PRAYING ABOUT

Ask God to help you tell each other the truth, to help you know when it's most loving to remain silent, and to heal wounds that may have been caused by a self-serving kind of "honesty."

WORTH DOING

Just for fun, tell each other something you don't remember revealing before (how much you really recall of your wedding ceremony, for instance). But ask yourself first whether this information will damage or build your relationship—and make sure it's the latter, not the former.

3

Helping Each Other
to Open Up

"An honest answer is like a kiss on the lips."
PROVERBS 24:26

Kim knew that when her husband came home he'd have an appetite for dinner. But what she hungered for was just a time to talk.

How will we ever get to know each other at this rate? I don't understand him any better than I did before our honeymoon.

When Matt came home, he kissed Kim and they sat down to eat. Kim launched into an animated account of her day. But Matt was his usual quiet self. He didn't seem to notice the favorite dinner she'd prepared. He silently chewed and nodded.

I shouldn't expect him to read my mind, she thought. *I'll just come right out and tell him what I want.* She explained as clearly as she could how much she needed him to open up.

Unfortunately, all Matt heard was criticism. He shot back that he already did so much for her. He worked long hours and provided well for them. They even prayed together. What more could she expect?

The evening ended on a sour note. They both knew they had a problem, and needed help.

As they told a counselor their stories, it became clear that Kim was having difficulty accepting the fact that Matt showed his love for her primarily through action—working hard—rather than by talking with her. As Matt listened to Kim, he began to realize that his actions weren't enough; they had to be accompanied by loving words that would speak to Kim's heart.

The counselor suggested a way to get conversation flowing between them. He called it "the Ten-Minute Plan."

The goal was to help Kim and Matt connect—in a way that fit their busy schedules. Three times a week, they were to spend four minutes reading a recommended marriage book together, four minutes having a positive discussion (no criticism), and two minutes praying. That was it—ten minutes of affirmation through reading, talking, listening, and praying, three times weekly.

It sounded easier than it turned out to be. But Kim and Matt didn't give up. Eventually the Ten-Minute Plan worked so well that they wanted more interaction—and more minutes together. They set aside time each week to do a routine task, giving them a comfortable context in which to talk even more.

By talking and listening, Kim and Matt found themselves more willing to open up to each other and adapt to each other's needs. Soon they knew each other better than ever.

As you try to get to know your spouse, is it hard for him or her to open up? Here are five principles to remember:

1. Communicate your need for conversation in a clear, respectful, forthright way; don't assume your spouse knows what you're thinking.

2. Notice when your spouse *does* try to talk with you. Express your appreciation for that with sincerity and kindness.

3. Commit yourselves to the Ten-Minute Plan of reading, talking, listening, and praying together. Don't give up even though it may be difficult at first.

4. Turn a routine activity into a time of conversation. For Kim and Matt it was cooking; for you and your spouse it could be anything from shopping to hiking to visiting garage sales.

5. Maintain a sense of humor about unexpected challenges in your conversations. Be patient and persistent.

As Kim and Matt found, it *is* possible to help a spouse open up. If it doesn't happen for you as quickly as it happened for them, keep at it!

—*James Groesbeck with Amy Swierczek*

WORTH THINKING ABOUT

Read Proverbs 24:26 again. Why is it important to answer a spouse's questions? How is responding to your mate's efforts at conversation like giving him or her a kiss?

WORTH PRAYING ABOUT

Ask God to show you any hurts or misunderstandings that may keep one or both of you from opening up. Thank Him that, by forgiving each other, you can start fresh—just as His compassion is new every morning (Lamentations 3:22-23).

WORTH DOING

Try the Ten-Minute Plan—ten minutes of affirmation through reading, talking, listening, and praying—three times this week. Then talk about how it went and whether you'd like to make it a habit.

4

Adjusting to Your Spouse's Personality

*"If the whole body were an eye, where would the
sense of hearing be? If the whole body were an
ear, where would the sense of smell be? But in fact
God has arranged the parts in the body, every
one of them, just as he wanted them to be."*

1 CORINTHIANS 12:17-18

"When she's stressed out, she talks all the time. If I get tired of talking to her after an hour or so, she gets a second wind and calls a friend!"

"He's so sensitive. I can't correct him without it making him angry. No matter what I say, he takes it wrong."

If these statements hit home, you're not alone. Most of us have said—or at least thought—similar things about our spouses.

Couples often tell therapists that one of their toughest challenges is adjusting to a spouse's personality. Many of those people are ready to give up and resign themselves to a miserable state of existence. Others fear their situations will worsen to a point where the spouse's personality turns repulsive—and divorce will be inevitable.

So what do you do? Stay miserable? Get angry and resentful? Leave?

We suggest none of the above.

Instead, consider these facts about differences in personalities.

1. *God created us to be different.* He knew there would be a place in His plan for introverts and extroverts, for thinkers and feelers. When we realize that, it's often easier to accept and adjust to a spouse's personality. It may even become possible to celebrate those differences. Otherwise, why would God create us in such variety—only to tell us to pair up and remain together for life? He's a God of compassion, not cruelty!

2. *It's easier to spot a flaw than to see a strength.* Jesus put it in terms of spying a speck in another's eye, versus seeing a log in our own (Matthew 7:3-5).

When you were dating, you probably found it easy to focus on the admirable traits of your future mate. You seemed to like the same things, enjoyed the same conversational topics, and tended to overlook each other's quirks.

Bennett, for instance, married Deb because she was such a "great communicator." Now he's annoyed because she's such a "great agitator." Dana married Marcus because he was such a "confident, strong manager." Now he's an "overconfident jerk."

3. *Your ability to tolerate your mate's personality changes with time.* Most of us can stand negative behavior for a while. But everyone has a limit!

Belinda, for example, could put up with Jeff's ability to make a joke out of everything—for about a year. After she became the brunt of his jokes, her level of tolerance changed. She reached a point where she despised his voice, especially his laughter.

Is that the case with you? Maybe it's not that your spouse's personality has become more of a problem; it may be that your ability to value or overlook some attributes has diminished. The change is in your "irritation threshold," which may need adjusting.

First Corinthians 12–14 urges us to appreciate individual differences. The apostle Paul explains that every member of the "body" is valuable. Just because a part is different doesn't give us the right to despise it and set it apart from the others.

The same is true with your mate's personality. It may be different and sometimes difficult to manage. But God doesn't want this to allow division in your marriage.

One of Paul's points to the Corinthians might be summarized this way: "Learn to accept and adjust to each other, no matter what people look like or act like." That applies to husbands and wives, too.

—*Mitch Temple*

WORTH THINKING ABOUT

Read 1 Corinthians 12:17-18 again. Is your spouse the eye, ear, brain, nose, hand, mouth, foot, spine, teeth, or muscle of your marriage? What would happen if you tried to take over that function?

WORTH PRAYING ABOUT

Thank God for two aspects of your spouse's personality that are different from yours.

WORTH DOING

Take a brief tour of your home together, looking for evidence of your own personality and that of your spouse. For example, your extroverted mate may have decorated a room with bright colors or lots of pictures of friends and family, or arranged chairs to form conversation areas. Find at least one positive thing to say about that trait and how it makes your life more interesting.

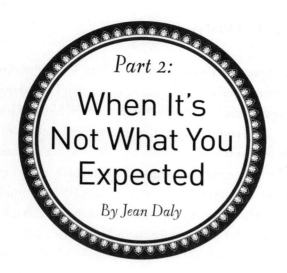

Jim and I were married August 24, 1986.

We started with a bang—lots of travel, the thrill of being newlyweds, and dreams of spending a lifetime together.

But then the train jumped the tracks.

We can't pinpoint the date when we reached rock bottom, but the dark clouds moved in sometime during our third year of marriage. I remember that night all too well. Jim had stepped into the bathroom to brush his teeth as we readied ourselves for bed. When he jumped under the covers, I was sobbing. Unsure what had provoked such heartfelt tears, he asked, "What's wrong?"

Brushing away the tears, I said, "I just don't think you should stay married to me."

Both of us had problems in our pasts that threatened to derail us from staying together. Our relationship was broken;

I felt distant and disconnected from Jim. I was wrestling with depression as well as a lack of confidence that I could overcome my struggles and be a good wife and mother. I knew God hated divorce, but I could not imagine us overcoming these struggles.

Jim had some of the same questions about himself. How could he be a good dad when he didn't have a solid example to follow? Jim loved his father—an unreliable gambler and alcoholic who threatened to harm Jim's mom with a hammer and was suicidal at one point in his life. Having divorced Jim's mother when Jim was just a child, the man hadn't taught Jim the first thing about how to love, cherish, or provide for a spouse.

Lying next to me that night, Jim said, "Jean, it seems to me that there are only two options for us, because divorce is not an option. We can do marriage one of two ways: happily or unhappily." He added, "With all of the stuff that's gone on in my life, I'd much rather do this happily."

We shared that bedrock of commitment, and it led us to get Christian counseling. We wish we'd had this book, too!

With help from trained professionals, we were ultimately able to begin untangling the difficulties in our background that kept us from winning at our marriage. As a result of seeking a counselor back then, our relationship today is stronger and more committed than ever. God has blessed us in ways we never dreamed He would.

We're hardly alone in discovering that marriage is rarely

what couples expect. We got off to a great start, but all was not rosy. We'd be the first to say that married life is hard work.

In that respect, our story is probably like that of millions of couples Focus on the Family serves. It's a story of love and fidelity that's framed by God's grace and mercy. When we stop long enough to connect the dots from our first conversation until this very morning, we see God's handiwork and purpose manifested in our marriage.

But we're also willing to admit we've still got our work cut out for us.

Has marriage brought you some surprises? Are you sometimes disappointed in your spouse or your circumstances? You'll find plenty to think, talk, and pray about in the section that follows.

5

Surprise!

"Plans fail for lack of counsel, but with
many advisers they succeed."

PROVERBS 15:22

On their honeymoon, Ed and Renee spent hours gazing into each other's eyes—contemplating how they'd spend their next 50 years. They decided to write those plans down as a road map for the future.

But before long, those plans hit several speed bumps.

Ed lost his job.

Renee was diagnosed with diabetes.

Habits that seemed cute at first became annoying.

When they had a son, Renee decided to stay home—which tightened the family purse strings. Ed worked more to compensate, further reducing their time together. When she voiced concern, it only seemed to irritate him.

They still loved each other. But this wasn't how either of them had written the script on their honeymoon.

You might find yourself wondering if *your* early dreams of

marital bliss were more illusion than reality. Why isn't marriage turning out the way you planned?

People draw their marital expectations from two wells. One is courtship. If dating was wonderful and starry-eyed, why would you expect marriage to be otherwise? *If spending 20 hours a week brings us such joy,* you might think, *more time together as husband and wife could only be better!*

But think back to your courtship. Wasn't it largely a mirage?

What did you do when you didn't want to be alone? You got dressed up and did fun things together. What did you do when you were tired of talking? You went home. How did you deal with financial decisions? You made them on your own.

When you were dating, there were some built-in escape valves in your relationship. Now that you're married, there's no other home to go to. Your spouse's finances are yours, and vice versa.

By its nature, courtship allows a couple to live in denial. Marriage makes that posture much more difficult to maintain.

The other well of marital expectations is the marriage you saw firsthand when you were growing up.

That relationship provided one of two images for you to view. Either the marriage didn't seem worth duplicating, or it did. But simply raising your expectations won't make your marriage better than that of your parents. You need to face past hurts and disappointments, perhaps with the help of a counselor or pastor. That may not have the same thrill that romance does, but it makes it more likely that you'll experience a fulfilling and romantic marriage.

You may have been fortunate enough to see a model of marriage worth replicating. For that you can rejoice! But there's a pitfall there, too. You may be locked into thinking that the way you saw Mom and Dad relate is the only healthy way for a marriage to function.

For example, let's say that your parents were both even-tempered; decisions came easily for them. You or your spouse might be more opinionated and need to discuss matters longer. That's okay, even though it's different. There are many styles in marriage that can be healthy.

If your expectations about marriage have been unrealistic, it's time to challenge them. But if you do, and still have concerns, consider the possibility that the problem might not be your expectations. You might have a problem in your marriage.

Harboring unrealistic expectations doesn't mean that everything else in a marriage is on track. Your qualms might be slightly off target, but they could be early warning signs about issues that will cause more trouble if you don't resolve them. Talk about them with your spouse in a respectful way; see whether the two of you can address them. If that fails, look to a pastor or counselor for help.

—*Glenn Lutjens*

WORTH THINKING ABOUT

Read Proverbs 15:22. Before you got married, what kind of "counsel" did you get from friends and family about what marriage would be like? How did it affect your expectations and plans?

WORTH PRAYING ABOUT

Ask God to help you have realistic expectations about marriage, and thank Him for the *pleasant* surprises that your spouse brings to your life.

WORTH DOING

Together, send a thank-you note or greeting card to parents or friends whose marriage has been a helpful model to you. Each of you can write a personal message naming at least one way in which that marriage has prepared you to face the unexpected.

6

"But I Thought My Spouse Was Perfect"

"To all perfection I see a limit; but your commands are boundless."

PSALM 119:96

Was your wife someone different before you got married? Has your husband changed for the worse over time?

It's much more likely that you saw your beloved through rose-colored glasses while you were dating, and now the glasses are off. And guess what? You're probably not the person he or she thought *you* were, either.

Before the wedding, differences tend to seem intriguing, interesting, and attractive. A few months or years into the marriage, however, what seemed so inviting in the semi-fantasy world of dating now seems considerably less than idyllic.

That beautiful angel you married turns out to be a real woman. That hunk has flaws that weren't previously apparent. Your mate may handle things in ways that you find inefficient, and isn't interested in your suggestions about how to do them differently—even though, from your viewpoint, your ways are obviously superior.

Perhaps your spouse has expectations you never guessed were there. You assumed they would match yours—and they don't.

How do these "mistakes" occur?

Barbie and Carl were so in love. They wanted to be with each other constantly. Unable to endure the thought of a long, drawn-out courtship, they married within three months of their first meeting.

Barbie was a life-of-the-party sort of girl—a social butterfly. A former high school cheerleader, she was bubbly and happy-go-lucky.

Carl was an A student in college. He had serious career plans in accounting and business. He liked books and challenging discussions about theology and politics. Not having dated many girls, he was in a daze when Barbie was willing to go out with him.

Barbie saw Carl as a responsible, mature man who'd provide stability and security. Carl saw Barbie as the perfect complement to his otherwise rather pedestrian life.

Two years into their marriage, though, there was a deep rift in their relationship. Carl was coming home from the office just wanting to read a book or have some quiet space. At bedtime he didn't feel very amorous.

Barbie seemed frustrated and angry when Carl had no

interest in dinner parties or going out dancing with her old friends. Going to church on Sunday mornings was more than enough social life for him.

Carl was angry and frustrated, too. Barbie was chronically late, ran up bills on the credit card, and was irresponsible about paying them.

What had gone so wrong with this relationship?

Carl and Barbie were opposites—and always had been. "Opposites attract" may be a common phenomenon but doesn't necessarily lead to a strong marriage. The mature and responsible guy seems to become a stiff, nit-picking perfectionist. The girl who appeared to be such a wonderful, bouncy, free spirit now looks like an irresponsible, immature twit.

If that's what's happened in your marriage, what should you do?

You might find it helpful to sit down and list the reasons why you chose this particular person to be your spouse. Think of all his or her attributes you enjoy and value. Think of yourself as the author of the Song of Songs, writing about your mate. Shift your focus from the negative and critical to the positive and appreciative.

Then make a date to share these thoughts with your spouse.

If this seems impossible, find a pastor or counselor to help you. Don't let disappointment make you vulnerable to the attentions of others. Don't consign yourself to regret and bitterness. Don't buy the lie that happiness lies just around the corner if only you escape from this "mistake" and move on to something new.

Your situation is not at all hopeless—if you get a fresh perspective on the imperfect person you married.

—Phillip J. Swihart

WORTH THINKING ABOUT

Read Psalm 119:96 again. If you and your spouse recognize each other's limits, how could that build your relationship? If the two of you recognize that God isn't limited, how could that strengthen your marriage?

WORTH PRAYING ABOUT

Ask God to help you see your spouse through His eyes this week.

WORTH DOING

Look together at a photo album, yearbook, home video, saved letters, or other record of your early days together. Reminisce about the things that attracted you to each other. Then, using Song of Songs 2 as a model, write each other notes about the attributes you enjoy and value in your spouse.

7

Why Isn't Your Spouse
More Like . . .

*"Accept one another, then, just as Christ accepted
you, in order to bring praise to God."*

ROMANS 15:7

Kevin was a smart guy. But, like many men, he made a mistake.

"Terri," he asked his wife, "why aren't you more like Mom?"

As you can imagine, Kevin didn't have time to explain himself. As soon as the words escaped his lips, Terri broke down in tears and ran out of the room, devastated.

Through the double-bolted door and between Terri's sobs, Kevin tried to explain what he really meant to say. He hadn't intended to hurt his wife. But he couldn't vindicate himself.

When you ask a question like that, you may be attempting to make a suggestion, "just something to consider." But your spouse probably wonders, *How can I compare to that?*

Many spouses, especially new ones, have made the "comparing mate to parent statement" or implied the same nonverbally. A wise person is one who can learn from and grow through his or her mistakes—or at least the mistakes of others. So, based on the experiences of spouses who have said the wrong thing, here are a few principles to remember.

1. *Comparing your spouse with others illuminates his or her flaws.* It's like painting a mole on your mate's face bright red; everybody will notice it.

Comparing your spouse to your parent puts your spouse in a position where he or she will fall short no matter what. Consider how unfair it would be for a wife to compare her new husband to her father. The latter might make twice the money the son-in-law did at his age, act as CEO of his own company, spend all his free time with his family, and serve as an elder in his church. No man could measure up to that kind of example. It would be like comparing Homer Simpson to Abraham.

Instead of comparing, try accepting and encouraging your mate. "Therefore encourage one another and build each other up, just as in fact you are doing" (1 Thessalonians 5:11).

2. *Learn to see your spouse through God's eyes.* God created David with distinctive strengths, yet David had obvious failings. In some ways he wouldn't have compared favorably with many ancient Israelites. Yet, with all his flaws, God said David was a man after His own heart.

We can be glad that God doesn't judge or place value on us by comparing our weakness to others' strengths. You can follow His example by valuing your spouse as the unique individual

God created him or her to be—not as a faint echo of your mom or dad.

3. *List and thank God for your spouse's good qualities.* If you've let yourself become nearsighted when it comes to seeing his or her good qualities, ask a mature Christian who knows both of you well to help you in this process. After you identify these qualities, talk to God about them. Thank Him for each attribute.

4. *Sing your mate's praises.* A "wife of noble character" is described in Proverbs 31. The author, King Lemuel, must have known the value of recognizing and extolling a spouse's good attributes. Note his final observation in verse 29: "Many women do noble things, but you surpass them all."

What a wise and compassionate man! If you insist on comparing your spouse to others, remember King Lemuel's example—and make sure you compare your mate in a positive way.

—*Mitch Temple*

WORTH THINKING ABOUT

Read Romans 15:7 again. Why does comparing a spouse unfavorably to a parent come across as rejection? What do you most need to accept about your mate in order to stop making such a comparison?

WORTH PRAYING ABOUT

Thank God for one of your spouse's strengths, for one of your parents' strengths, and for the opportunity to benefit from both.

WORTH DOING

If your parents are living, think of a favor you and your spouse can do for them—using your unique skills. You might cook a special meal for them, sing them a song over the phone, or help them understand how to use a smartphone or tablet. If your parents have passed away, use your unique skills to do a favor for someone else—in their memory.

8

Did You Marry the Wrong Person?

"Love . . . always protects, always trusts,
always hopes, always perseveres."

1 CORINTHIANS 13:6-7

The late movie star Mickey Rooney said, "Marriage is like batting in baseball; when the right one comes along, you don't want to let it go by." It sounds good, until you realize that Mickey was married eight times. He must have had a lot of "good pitches" to swing at!

Perhaps he held what might be called the "needle in a haystack" view of picking a mate. According to this perspective, there's only one spouse with whom you could be happy. That person needs to be found even if it means discarding a spouse who no longer looks right for you.

Significant emotional pain lies in the wake of such a view. You won't find a "wrong needle" clause in the Bible that gives you an "out" if you conclude that your spouse isn't right for you.

Instead you'll find in Malachi 2:15, "Do not break faith with the wife of your youth."

Marriage is not primarily about *finding* the right spouse. It's about *being* the right person.

If you and your loved one were unhappy as singles and expected marriage to fulfill your lives, you probably were greatly disappointed as your level of contentment dropped even lower. But if you sensed meaning and purpose in your lives individually and wanted to share them in a lifetime commitment, you likely experienced an increase in contentment. You might call this the Mine Theory of Mate Selection. You either find the "land mine" or the "gold mine" in marriage.

During courtship, people are often sure they've found the "gold mine." Both spouses-to-be tend to get excited about this wonderful, new relationship. The fireworks of romance help them act kinder, more selflessly, and more empathetically than they might when the fire fades.

We tend to fill in the gaps regarding the person we love. We assume during courtship that since he's willing to sit and listen to our feelings about life, he'll show the same concern after marriage when we want to talk about our frustrations. When he doesn't, we assume we married the wrong person.

In reality, he probably was not as wonderful as you thought he was before you married. On the other hand, he's probably not as terrible as you might now be thinking.

In his classic work, *The Art of Loving*, Erich Fromm

declares, "To love somebody is not just a strong feeling—it is a decision, it is a judgment, it is a promise. If love were just a feeling, there would be no basis for the promise to love each other forever."[2]

When the two of you walked down the aisle, each of you became the right person for the other. Yes, you may look back and second-guess your reasons. But you entered an arena in which learning to truly love someone takes a lifetime.

That's what Larry and Linda learned.

When they entered counseling, Larry assumed he'd made a mistake by marrying Linda. But he came to understand that learning to love her was helping him grow as a spouse and become more lovable. He might not have married Linda, knowing what he now knows about her. Yet he recognizes that beyond human decisions, God somehow works His purposes into the equation.

Larry no longer views marriage with a "needle in a haystack" mentality. He considers Linda as the one he's promised to love both in sickness and in health.

—*Glenn Lutjens*

WORTH THINKING ABOUT

Read 1 Corinthians 13:6-7 again. Which requires more protecting, trusting, hoping, and persevering: *finding* the right spouse or *being* the right spouse? Why?

WORTH PRAYING ABOUT

Ask God to help each of you to *be* the right person for one another.

WORTH DOING

Talk about the following phrases spouses sometimes use: "We're soulmates"; "God made you for me"; "Our marriage was made in heaven"; "You're the one for me." Do they reflect a "needle in a haystack" outlook? Do they have some truth to them? Do you need to replace them with other phrases or just think of them differently?

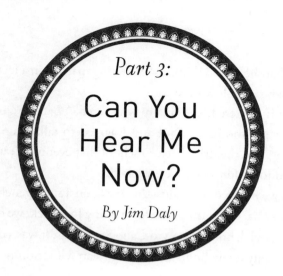

Part 3:

Can You Hear Me Now?

By Jim Daly

Somebody once suggested that opposites attract—but it's the like-minded that last. As a couple with very different temperaments, Jean and I would certainly agree.

Shortly after we were engaged we found ourselves having dinner on a Sunday night at my brother's house. The phone rang. The call was from an Australian business friend named Paul. He had an interesting opportunity and wondered if I knew anyone who might be interested. PepsiCo was sponsoring a drug and alcohol awareness program for high schools across America. They needed a two-person team to emcee the presentation, run the video equipment, and talk with students.

I blurted out, "How about Jean and me?"

He paused. "You'd have to be married," he said dismissively.

I excused myself, put my hand over the receiver, and asked

Jean what she would think about getting married in a few weeks so as to be eligible for the gig.

A bit flustered, she finally whispered, "Can we give him an answer tomorrow?" Paul and I agreed to talk again in the morning. On the drive back to school that evening, Jean and I decided to go for it. We were excited!

So we married on August 24, 1986, on a sun-drenched day in Santa Ana, California. Due for training in a week, we decided to take a quick honeymoon to Cabo San Lucas. It was a disaster! Within only a few hours of arriving, Jean fell seriously ill. She passed out in the hotel room.

I panicked. Was this it? Would I be a widower within a day of our wedding? I ran to get the doctor. Jean was as white as the sheets she was lying on. Fortunately, by the time the doctor arrived, she'd regained consciousness. But by the next day I caught what Jean had, and wound up shivering my way through a dangerous fever for the rest of our honeymoon. All we did for the whole week was hold hands!

For the next nine months we visited over 100 high schools in 17 states. I loved it.

And Jean? Not nearly as much as I did.

We spent every waking minute together—a dream come true for an extrovert, but a challenge for someone like my dear wife who craves her quiet time. When Jean excused herself one evening to buy some groceries, I clamored to go along.

"No! No! It's OK!" she said in exasperation. "I got it!"

Differences. When it comes to marriage, we can't live with 'em and we can't live without 'em. That's especially true when it comes to communicating as couples.

One of my favorite guests on our daily broadcast is popular author and child psychologist Dr. Kevin Leman. On a recent program Dr. Leman began by explaining that the average marriage lasts just seven years. According to his experience mentoring couples, one of the primary reasons marriages get in trouble is a failure to understand and appreciate the fact that men are men and women are women. The sexes simply have different ways of communicating, relating, and viewing the world. While that seems so intuitive on the surface, practically speaking, it's not.

To illustrate the different ways men and women approach communication, Dr. Leman announced he'd pre-recorded a conversation with Jean. I felt busted! I immediately looked over at my co-host, John Fuller. Was he in on the conspiracy? Turns out John had no idea where things were headed, either. In fact, Dr. Leman had spoken with John's wife, too. We both started to sweat right there in the studio!

Thankfully, I married up when I married Jean. I'd say she was gracious in the way she described how we used to misfire in the area of communication. With my heart pounding just a little faster, Jean's voice filled the speakers. She recalled a time about seven years into our marriage when she had something important she wanted to tell me. The moment she picked to talk and "connect" with me just happened to be in the middle of a football game. I think you might know where this is going.

Jean said, "Jim liked to watch football Sunday afternoons and Monday nights. From my perspective, what a great time to connect. He's just sitting there and it's just football, right? So I would start having conversations with him. I remember actually feeling hurt that Jim was ignoring me."

In fairness, that's an understatement. Jean wasn't just a little bit hurt. This was a big deal for her. All she wanted was to interact with her husband and enjoy my company. I, however, was too focused on the game. Why? I'm a guy, so it wasn't "just football." Watching a game was how I unwound after a crazy day of work. That's a big difference in how many men and women view sports and the need for conversation.

To her credit, Jean started using a new approach to spanning our communication gap. As she told Dr. Leman, "I would go to Jim and say, 'Is this a good time to ask you something?' and then allow Jim to be able to say, 'Well, they're just about ready to score. Can it wait a minute?' I've also learned that a football minute isn't a real minute—but that's okay. I've also learned not to discuss heavy, deep issues during football games."

Now, after years of practice, when Jean asks me that question—"Is this a good time to ask you something?"—a light goes on in my head. It reminds me that I either need to stop what I'm doing, turn and face her, and give her my full attention—or at least be honest enough to say, "Well, now isn't the best time, but I look forward to talking after dinner." In turn, Jean has learned to trust me when I say that not being able to converse at the moment doesn't mean that I'm disinterested in her world.

One of the most beautifully mysterious elements of a godly marriage is how the Lord can bring together two distinctly different people and form them into one flesh (Genesis 2:24). But it only works if we're committed to fully appreciating one another's uniqueness. That's what the following section is about.

9

When One of You Is the Silent Type

*"Greater love has no one than this, that
he lay down his life for his friends."*
JOHN 15:13

Carl is overwhelmed by Betsy's need for conversation. It feels like a void that can never be filled. It's decreasing his desire to be intimate with her; he's finding excuses to avoid even spending time together.

Betsy longs for the Carl she knew before they got married—the one who couldn't seem to stop talking nor get enough of her. She was so excited back then, and believed it would go on forever. Now she feels duped.

Maybe you do, too. Maybe you fear your uncommunicative spouse isn't interested in you, isn't excited about you, or doesn't love you anymore. You might doubt that you married the right person—or feel inadequate, insecure, and desperate for attention.

When that happened to Betsy, she changed, too. Now Carl

finds himself wondering what happened to the self-assured, strong woman he first fell in love with. He misses her.

Carl doesn't realize it, but Betsy has always had an unusual need for attention and communication. That's because she had a very stoic father whom she was never able to please.

Relating to each other isn't a skill we're born with. It's like a muscle that needs to be developed over time. If you have a spouse who doesn't want to talk as much as you do, try the following suggestions.

1. *Read about the differences between men and women, especially as they relate to communication.* You may discover why your spouse tends to be the silent type.

2. *Learn to not take things too personally.* In Betsy's case, her need to talk was influenced by her relationship with her father, not just her relationship with Carl.

3. *Don't overanalyze your partner.* You may think you know what's behind your spouse's unwillingness to talk, but you can't read his or her mind.

4. *Talk about your feelings in a non-accusatory, non-blaming way.* To do otherwise will only drive a reluctant talker further away, especially when it comes to discussing emotions.

5. *Ask your spouse what would make him feel less overwhelmed when it comes to communication.* Would it help if you set aside a regular time for talking? If you waited until he decompressed after work?

6. *Ask your spouse for a specific, short commitment of time.* Most reluctant talkers can handle a conversation if they know it won't last forever. Let your mate set the limit. You may find that it increases as he or she grows more comfortable.

7. *Learn each other's personality type, and how it shapes communication style.* Make the process fun—a discovery of your uniqueness, not an opportunity to stereotype each other.

Betsy wanted to confess her feelings of hopelessness to Carl about their situation. But she knew she had to do it in a loving and safe environment. One evening she served his favorite meal, then later tucked the children into bed. Then she talked.

His reaction encouraged her. He expressed his support for their marriage and his love for her, which helped her understand that his silence wasn't caused by a lack of caring. Carl revealed how the demands for conversation affected him, and the ways in which he may have been withdrawing for self-protection.

Carl promised to start using a short daily devotional book with Betsy. The two of them set up a plan for a bi-weekly date night. They also decided to learn more about healthy communication.

Betsy and Carl recommitted themselves to their marriage. They promised each other that, instead of giving up, they would get help if they needed it.

—*Romie Hurley*

WORTH THINKING ABOUT

Read John 15:13 again. What sacrifices did Betsy and Carl need to make in order to build a satisfying line of communication? When it comes to conversation, what sacrifice might mean the most to your spouse?

WORTH PRAYING ABOUT

Ask God for the wisdom to know when to sacrifice your own communication needs and preferences for the sake of your spouse.

WORTH DOING

Make a list of five questions or conversation starters to use with your spouse this week. Keep track of the results in a journal. Pay attention to whether some topics inspire more conversation than others. Make a note of questions that cause your spouse to change the subject or clam up. Based on your observations, create a better-targeted list to use the following week.

IO

When One of You Won't Stop Talking

"A time to tear and a time to mend, a time to be silent and a time to speak..."
ECCLESIASTES 3:7

Bill is avoiding his wife, Carol.

He knows he's doing it, and he feels guilty about it. But he thinks it's the only way to deal with his predicament.

He can't seem to handle her frequent demands for conversation. He feels that she nags him continually. When he just wants to relax, she has another emotional outburst about how he never talks to her.

Bill hasn't told Carol exactly how he feels about all this. He doesn't want her to get angry or hurt.

But Carol is already both of those things. She can't believe Bill chose once again to spend Saturday golfing with his buddies. She was looking forward to spending the day with him, hoping they could find some of the closeness they once shared.

She feels rejected. The more he avoids talking with her, the more insecure she feels and the harder she tries to get him to "open up."

If you're feeling nagged to talk, you're probably feeling overwhelmed, too. Avoidance may seem like the only solution for relief. This relief is only temporary, though, because it leaves your spouse without resolution—and often determined to try harder.

Here are some suggestions if you're feeling cornered by a spouse who always seems to be asking, "Can we talk?"

1. Take the initiative to spend time doing things together *other* than talking.
2. Find a Christian book about communication in marriage. Read from it aloud to your spouse and ask her questions about her reactions.
3. Share a chore, like doing the dishes. You may find yourself communicating during the dull moments.
4. When she's not expecting it, ask, "How can I show you I love you?" or "What would make your day easier?"
5. Put the newspaper away, neglect a hobby, or shut the TV off in order to spend time with your spouse.
6. Keep a sense of humor. Find cartoons about how different men and women are, and how they communicate. Make more fun of your own gender than the other person's.

These are all good things to do, but it's also important for you to ask for the peace and quiet you may need. Otherwise, you'll probably feel like a helpless victim of your mate's demands.

One way to do this is to set a specific time to talk. This should thrill your spouse, since it represents a commitment to communicate. The limits need to be spelled out, though, in order to avoid false expectations.

Try 20 or 30 minutes to start. Get a kitchen timer and stick to the limit. What should you do during that time? Here are some ideas.

- Explore and discuss your needs for communication.
- Explore and discuss your needs for quiet or alone time.
- Explore and discuss your needs for outside friendships and recreation.
- Use "I" statements to convey feelings of being pressured, overwhelmed, or discouraged. This will help keep your spouse from feeling attacked. For example: "I feel hopeless when I hear 'We need to talk,' because it reminds me of my mom. She always used that phrase when I was in trouble."

If Bill and Carol follow these suggestions, Bill likely will feel more in control, seeing how to give Carol what she needs without fearing it will never be enough. He'll grow more assertive in asking for what he needs, and less guilty about taking time for himself.

Carol will feel less threatened, emotional, and needy. She'll be happier, more content. She'll know Bill loves her because he's been initiating doing things together—and even asking about her feelings.

—*Romie Hurley*

WORTH THINKING ABOUT

Read Ecclesiastes 3:7 again. Why is silence important? Why does it have its limits, especially in a relationship?

WORTH PRAYING ABOUT

Thank God for giving us seasons of life, as described in Ecclesiastes 3. Ask Him to help you establish a rhythm of silence and talking in your relationship that works for both of you.

WORTH DOING

Invite friends over to play Pictionary, charades, or some other game that requires communication without talking. Make sure you and your spouse are partners. Afterward, discuss how good you were at communicating without talking. Compare it to how good you are communicating by talking. Keep the discussion lighthearted. If you're comfortable with the idea, ask your friends to offer their input—without taking sides.

11

Learning Each Other's Language

*"So God created man in his own image,
in the image of God he created him;
male and female he created them."*

GENESIS 1:27

Are men and women really from different planets? When it comes to communication, it sometimes seems that way.

Men tend to use language to transmit information, report facts, fix problems, clarify status, and establish control. Women are more likely to view language as a means to greater intimacy, stronger or richer relationships, and fostering cooperation rather than competition.

Those differences can easily lead to distorted conclusions about the other person's motivations.

She's an unreasonable, demanding nag who won't leave me alone to watch the football game, he thinks.

He's an insensitive, domineering bore who doesn't have a clue about my feelings and doesn't want one, she tells herself.

Nancy and Ralph are having this kind of conflict.

Nancy sits in the counselor's office in tears. Ralph, her husband of three years, sits stony-faced, two feet away on the same couch.

She begins the session with a litany of Ralph's alleged failures, the worst being his neglect of her needs. He is, she says, "never home." Self-employed, he works long hours and takes frequent business trips. He also leaves her with the care of their one-year-old.

When he's home, she says, he's either restoring an antique car or wanting to jump into bed for a quick sexual romp—for which he seems to have plenty of energy. When she's dead tired and turns him down, he pouts and sometimes storms out to the garage and his beloved Chevy. She notes with undisguised sarcasm that he's always too tired to just talk to her.

The final straw: Last week, on her birthday, he was gone on another business trip. She feels abandoned and unloved.

When Ralph finally speaks up, it's to say that things are usually much more peaceful in the garage than in the bedroom. At least the Chevy doesn't treat him like he's some dirty old man.

He can't understand why Nancy is so angry about his long hours at work. She seems to him to have no concept of what it takes to earn the money needed each month to pay the bills. This is how a husband and father takes care of—loves—his family.

Standing outside looking in, it seems easy to see that when it comes to understanding each other's languages, Nancy and Ralph are missing each other by a mile. In many respects, they exemplify stereotypical male-female struggles with differences in communication.

If, like too many couples, you enter marriage focused on *being* loved rather than on *giving* love, you may experience similar communication problems. Try making it your goal not to change your spouse but to adapt to his or her style of communication. Turn your attention to hearing the heart of your partner rather than to the frustration you may feel about not being heard or understood.

This is not a hopeless situation. In fact, compared to many marital conflicts, it's a state that can more quickly and remarkably improve—when two children of God who are committed to their marriage decide to work on it and seek appropriate help.

—*Phillip J. Swihart*

WORTH THINKING ABOUT

Read Genesis 1:27 again. Why are men and women so radically different when both are created in God's image? What attributes of God do many women reflect? What attributes do many men reflect?

WORTH PRAYING ABOUT

Ask the Creator to help you recognize His image when you interact with your spouse—and to treat him or her accordingly.

WORTH DOING

Make a date with each other once a week to try a communication exercise. For ten minutes one of you will talk about feelings or issues you have; the other will do nothing but listen. He or she may respond only with, "I don't understand; could you restate that?" or "What I hear you saying is . . ." When time's up, the other person will get ten minutes to talk. At the end of the exercise, neither of you is allowed to try to "straighten the other one out," react angrily to something you didn't want to hear, or debate the issue.

12

How to Connect Without Talking

*"A man of knowledge uses words with restraint,
and a man of understanding is even-tempered.
Even a fool is thought wise if he keeps silent,
and discerning if he holds his tongue."*

PROVERBS 17:27-28

When Paige and her husband, Steve, sit down to talk, she's usually intimidated. She knows Steve loves her, but he hardly ever smiles. *Is he mad at me?* she wonders.

Cherie doesn't understand why her husband, Brian, got so upset yesterday when she left him a Post-It note on the kitchen table. She was just reminding him to take out the trash. Would he have been happier if she'd drawn a little smiley face on it?

Unspoken communication—a raised eyebrow, a folding of the arms across the chest, a hand on the shoulder, an e-mail—can be at least as powerful as talking. It can help build your marriage—or chip away at it.

Communicating without talking can be tricky. You may not always realize what you're "saying." And your silent messages may contradict your spoken ones, confusing your spouse.

The unspoken can be very difficult to interpret properly. Nevertheless, nonverbal communication has its positive side. To help you and your mate make the most of those silent messages, here are some principles to remember:

1. *Go low-tech when possible.* When it comes to communicating with your spouse, don't try to send important messages or work out sensitive issues over the phone or via e-mail.

When you read an e-mail or listen on the phone, you're not getting the whole message. You can't interpret facial expressions, maintain eye contact, or sense warmth or genuineness. If intimate, relationship-building conversation is needed, have it face-to-face.

2. *Don't be "all talk."* Actions speak louder than words. You can tell a hungry man you care about him and wish him well, but if you don't demonstrate your compassion the words are useless. The same is true for your spouse.

3. *Don't rely on silence to send a message.* Silence can be one of the loudest forms of communication, but it's easily misinterpreted. The trouble with silence is that your mate may "fill in the blanks" with answers that aren't correct. Learning to communicate what you feel will help your spouse know what's in

your heart—instead of encouraging him or her to take your silence and assume the worst.

4. *Don't catastrophize.* In other words, don't overreact. What you *think* your spouse meant may not be what he or she intended to communicate.

Ask for clarification: "Remember the other day when I asked you about taking a vacation and you sighed real loud? Were you aggravated with me because I brought it up again, or were you frustrated with yourself for having forgotten about it?"

5. *Watch your body language.* Your facial expressions and eye contact send messages to your spouse about how interested you are in what he or she is saying. Actions like looking away, cleaning your fingernails, yawning, or flipping channels on the remote say, "I have better things to do."

6. *Use touch to communicate your love.* Spouses who fail to affectionately touch each other by holding hands, rubbing necks, putting their arms around each other, and hugging will not be as close—literally and figuratively—as those who make these patterns part of their everyday routine.

7. *Use your eyes to express warmth and caring.* In marriage, your eyes can communicate affection or disgust, contentment or dissatisfaction, love or hatred, approval or disappointment. Make a habit of looking your spouse in the eyes, especially when you're discussing sensitive topics or expressing love.

—*Mitch Temple*

WORTH THINKING ABOUT

Read Proverbs 17:27-28 again. Why is silence often associated with wisdom? In what situations is silence not a wise choice?

WORTH PRAYING ABOUT

Ask God to make your heart sensitive to your spouse's communication needs, and to give you the wisdom to know when to speak and when to stay silent.

WORTH DOING

Once a day for the next week, try to guess what your spouse is thinking. Find a moment when he or she seems relaxed and say, "I'll bet you're thinking about _____." Depending on your mood, you can fill in the blank with a legitimate guess or something that will make your spouse laugh. If you take a lighthearted approach, you'll find that your guesses can be great conversation starters.

Part 4:

Your
Love Life

By Jim Daly

A recent issue of *Reader's Digest* grabbed my attention. Splashed across the front cover was the following question: "Is Your Marriage Normal or Nuts?" When I flipped to the article, it promised to share the "8 Lessons from the World's Happiest Couples."

Naturally, I was intrigued. Jean and I would consider ourselves part of a happy marriage. But could we vouch for all eight of these "lessons"?

The list was fairly predictable. Happily married couples are kind to each other and talk regularly about all kinds of things. They also avoid going to bed angry.

But then, speaking of bed, this one really jumped out at me: According to the experts associated with the *Reader's Digest* study, 60 percent of extremely happy couples have sex three or four times per week.

I had to read that statistic again.

And then I wanted to make sure I shared it with Jean!

Based on 27 years of marital experience, I knew exactly what she'd say in response to such a finding. Care to guess? Undoubtedly she would have noted that the majority of the women in the study were not mothers of young children, which she is. It's not that moms of youngsters aren't interested in sexual intimacy—it's just that the minute they lie down they're likely to fall asleep out of sheer exhaustion!

So I decided not to show the magazine to Jean. It would have been unfair. In this season of life, Jean is going a hundred miles an hour. From sunup to sundown she's investing in the lives of our young boys.

Still, intimacy doesn't have to be a casualty of the daily grind. Authors Bill and Pam Farrel, frequent and popular guests on the *Focus on the Family* radio program, are especially adept at guiding couples through the challenging waters of sexual intimacy and helping each other set and adjust expectations. Consider what they recently wrote:

> [As married couples] we must make a choice regarding sexual expression. We will either utilize it as a deviant, destructive power or we will harness its potential to keep love alive and vibrant in our marriage relationships. In a marriage, sex is the spice that rescues our relationships from becoming mundane pursuits of chores. Adult life

is filled with responsibilities. We have mortgages to pay, yard work to maintain, laundry to clean, cars to service, and so on. But none of us got married so we could load up on chores. We got married out of hope. We got married because we believed there was some kind of magic between us. We got married because we believed we could have great sex together.

A satisfying sex life can add dignity to all other pursuits of life. It is the thing to look forward to after a dull or miserable day at work. Sex is the moment of connection that creates a deep bond, even when sprinkled weeks or months apart. Sexual union adds an underlying deposit of strength that can help hold couples together when life threatens to pull them apart.[3]

They're absolutely right!

In the following pages you're going to find some terrific and timely counsel on this very subject. It may be one you haven't talked much about as a couple. We hope you'll relax, keep your sense of humor, share as honestly as you can, listen to each other carefully, and prayerfully consider the guidance offered.

13

What Does He Want from You?

"May your fountain be blessed, and may you rejoice in the wife of your youth. A loving doe, a graceful deer—may her breasts satisfy you always, may you ever be captivated by her love."

PROVERBS 5:18-19

Julie watched the attractive women at her husband's office party and felt an unfamiliar pang of worry.

Derek was naturally outgoing, and that ability to connect with others had been a big factor in his success in sales. A devoted Christian, he'd never given her reason to doubt his fidelity. But it was obvious women noticed him.

What was it the expert on that talk show had said? "If you don't romance your husband, someone else will."

Julie shivered. Their sex life had been declining since their honeymoon three years earlier. She'd never really understood what had gone wrong.

Women are often characterized as mysterious and men as

more basic and straightforward. But one-dimensional stereo-types only take us so far. Men can be inscrutable, too—and a wife who wants to be a good sexual partner looks for keys to unlock his mysteries as well.

Here are five steps toward being the partner your husband wants.

1. *Be secure in your own sexuality.* Instead of leaving him to guess your needs and preferences, speak candidly and without criticizing. Many husbands wish their wives would more often initiate sex. Find out how he likes to be approached and add that to the menu occasionally.

2. *Affirm his masculinity.* There are non-sexual ways to affirm your husband, too. In private, you either build or diminish his confidence in the way you regard his interests, hobbies, parent-ing skills, and friendships. Showing respect for the things that are important to him directly affects your whole relationship.

You should also consider how you talk to others about him. Criticism or barbed jests shoot down intimacy on every level. Conversely, placing your hand on his hand or shoulder tells him and others, "This man is mine, and I'm glad."

3. *Give him freedom of access.* A husband's feeling of having to "beg" for sex is too common a complaint to omit. If you find yourself frequently making excuses, figure out what's behind that pattern. Do your part to identify and eliminate the barri-ers that keep you from enjoying sex, so you can be a receptive, enthusiastic partner.

4. Understand his sexual needs. Testosterone causes your husband to desire and think about sex more than you do. Most men desire sex at least three times a week and think of it more often than that.

While you shouldn't blindly force yourself to serve him sexually whether you feel like it or not, at least start by asking him what his needs are. Your discussion should assure him that you understand his needs and care about meeting them.

5. Help him stay faithful. A man's visually-oriented arousal mechanism is part of God's purposeful design. The fact that your husband delights in how you look, feel, and smell can be a source of enjoyment for you both. Paying general attention to how you keep yourself is an important part of his sensory experience.

Driving home from the office party, Julie took a deep breath. "Derek," she said, "I want to make sure I'm meeting your needs as a wife."

Derek's eyes widened. "You mean sexually?"

"Well, yeah. Those women obviously noticed you. I just want to make sure you feel satisfied."

Derek gently squeezed her hand. "I know we have some things to work on, but I'm very satisfied with you."

Julie sighed. "I want you to tell me if there are things you wish were different or better."

Derek nodded.

We might not be there yet, Julie thought. *But it's a start.*

—*Rob Jackson*

WORTH THINKING ABOUT

Read Proverbs 5:18-19 again. Why do God and His Word often get accused of being anti-sex? How would you summarize God's actual attitude toward human sexuality?

WORTH PRAYING ABOUT

Thank God for His gift of sexuality, and ask Him to help you use it in ways that honor Him and satisfy you and your spouse.

WORTH DOING

Remember together the first 24 hours of your marriage. Talk candidly with your spouse about the excitement, the nervousness, and the anticipation of your first night together as husband and wife. Be as open, frank, and romantic as possible. Complete this thought for your spouse: "If I'd known then what I know now about you, here's what I would have done differently that night."

14

What Does She Want from You?

"Each of you should look not only to your own interests, but also to the interests of others."

PHILIPPIANS 2:4

"Do you want to talk about it?" Evan's voice was flat, his eyes unable to meet Anna's.

"Yeah, I guess," she said, and shrugged.

Last night had been hard for both of them. After two and a half years of marriage, they seemed to have reached a dead end, sexually speaking. They'd tried new things, but it was a hit-or-miss process. Even when he tried to please her the way she suggested, he never seemed to get it right. They both just ended up frustrated.

What does your wife want from her sexual relationship with you? Here are four things to consider.

1. *Romance.* A woman's need for emotional intimacy to precede physical intimacy is at the heart of what we call romance.

Romance can mean something different to each individual, but the common factor for most women involves a feeling of being valued. Become a student of your wife at the physical, emotional, mental, and spiritual levels. Ask her what she enjoys sexually. Find out what makes her feel cherished. Strive to be the world's greatest expert on her.

2. *Non-sexual touch.* Men often like overtly sexual advances, but most women say they prefer a more relational approach. Your non-sexual touch throughout the day tells your wife you value her as being much more than just an object of desire. If the only time you touch her is when you want sex, the inadvertent message you send is that you want to use her body rather than loving her whole person.

3. *Intimacy.* For most wives, emotional intimacy must precede physical intimacy. Respect, safety, and friendship are essential to unlocking her heart. If you habitually criticize or make barbed jokes about her, you'll find she's not responsive sexually when she feels unsafe emotionally.

4. *Purity.* A wife's sense of emotional safety depends on how much she can trust you. This isn't limited to sexual fidelity. She needs to see you being voluntarily accountable for your time, your money, your eyes, and every other aspect of your life. In other words, show her she can entrust herself to you.

A second part of her need for your purity is your role in her spiritual nurture. Servant leadership in the home carries out

God's intended role for the husband to be a picture of Christ. Just as Christ laid down His life for His bride, the church, take every opportunity to pour out your life for her sake (see Ephesians 5:25-31). When your wife sees you growing, serving, and leading spiritually, it frees her to give herself to you in every way, including sexually.

Those four principles apply to most wives. But what about yours?

When you get right down to it, there's only one way to find out what your wife really wants. Ask her.

That means honest conversation, even if it's a little uncomfortable at first. Here are Evan and Anna again, trying to get that conversation going.

"I just felt so awkward last night," Anna says. "I always imagined sex would be easy, like a romantic movie. You know, where the characters just fall into each others' arms and automatically know what to do without any words."

Evan nods, relieved that they're finally getting things into the open. "Me, too. Those movies leave you thinking there isn't anything confusing or messy." He pauses. "I think we just need to say what we're thinking and wanting. If something doesn't work, we can figure it out together."

Anna shrugs again, but this time with a smile. "I guess. We're a good team on everything else. Why not this, too?"

—*Rob Jackson*

WORTH THINKING ABOUT

Read Philippians 2:4 again. What are some challenges that result from men and women being wired differently, sexually speaking? Why is unselfishness—looking to the interest of another—important in meeting those challenges?

WORTH PRAYING ABOUT

Ask God to help you develop an unselfish attitude toward physical intimacy, a desire to put the wants and needs of your spouse ahead of your own.

WORTH DOING

Describe an ideal romantic encounter with your partner. Include as many specific details as possible. Where would it take place? What time of day would it be? What would the circumstances be? Make sure you touch on as many things as possible that would enhance your romantic mood.

15

Moving Beyond the Past

*"He heals the brokenhearted and
binds up their wounds."*

PSALM 147:3

Julie thought sex was something dirty that had ruined her life. She took no pleasure in intimacy with her husband.

Her plight had its roots in her childhood. That was when her father had abused her sexually. The experience had repulsed her, but at the same time proved she had something men desired. When she got to college, she was sexually promiscuous.

When a dysfunctional sexual past haunts you, it usually haunts your spouse—and your whole relationship.

It's not supposed to be that way, of course. Sex is a beautiful gift from God, intended to mirror the spiritual union between His people and Himself.

Many struggle with guilt from wrong sexual choices they've made. Others are bitter over wrong choices made by an abuser. Still others wrestle with anger over wrong choices a spouse has made in having an affair.

If you're suffering from the fallout of your sexual past, here are some things you need to know.

1. *Unresolved hurt from your sexual past disrupts healthy sexual functioning.* Surveys indicate that many people have been pressured into a sexual act at some point. The emotions accompanying that event are often too intense to process. Hurt and confusion may be mixed with excitement. The violated person may sense that something isn't quite right, but dismisses the feeling because the perpetrator showed interest in him or her.

Many caught in this bind are also sworn to secrecy, often threatened with harm. Others fear that they will be blamed. Most carry the false burden of guilt that they were somehow responsible for the offense.

Consensual sex prior to, or outside of, marriage may also influence your sexual functioning now. Pregnancy, abortion, sexually transmitted diseases, and the bonds formed through sexual relationships can trigger emotional distress for years.

2. *Problems are opportunities to draw closer to God.* A troubled sexual past may look insurmountable, but it's not—if you run toward God instead of away from Him.

God designed life to be more than we can manage on our own. More than anything else, He wants us to come to Him to be made whole again. Only a relationship with Him through Christ can set us free from guilt and anger.

3. *God wants to heal the deep hurts of the sexual past.* As

ointment is applied to heal an injury, the power of God must be personally applied to each wounding of the human spirit.

The first step in sexual healing is gaining the courage to face your pain. This process may be time consuming, and may require the help of others. Because broken trust is always involved at some level, you must deal simultaneously with two things you most fear: recalling the trauma and being vulnerable to be hurt again.

4. *Core beliefs, thoughts, and feelings affect present sexual behavior.* Outward behavior is the tip of an iceberg dominated by underlying emotions, thoughts, and core beliefs. Great freedom comes from understanding these factors and the deeper assumptions that drive them.

5. *Professional help is often needed to resolve past sexual hurts.* Under the guidance of the Holy Spirit and with the help of qualified therapists, many come to experience profound emotional healing. This includes breaking long-standing, destructive behavior patterns.

That was the case with Julie. She told her husband that problems from her sexual past were keeping her from enjoying intimacy with him.

The two of them were referred to a Christian counselor who specialized in healing sexual hurts. Julie learned how to correct the underlying beliefs and thought patterns that triggered her painful emotions, much to the benefit of her marriage.

—*James Vigorito*

WORTH THINKING ABOUT

Read Psalm 147:3 again. How does God heal wounds that aren't physical? What does emotional healing feel like?

WORTH PRAYING ABOUT

Ask God to give you the wisdom and courage to deal with the obstacles that prevent you from enjoying sexual intimacy with your spouse, and ask Him to help you experience His healing.

WORTH DOING

Buy two copies of a Christian book on sexual intimacy in marriage. Read the book individually, highlighting passages that you believe relate specifically to your relationship. After both of you have finished, compare the passages you highlighted. Discuss the areas in which you agree and in which you differ, and decide what your next step as a couple should be.

16

Where Did Our Love Life Go?

"The husband should fulfill his marital duty to his wife,
and likewise the wife to her husband. The wife's body does
not belong to her alone but also to her husband. In the same
way, the husband's body does not belong to him alone but
also to his wife. Do not deprive each other except by mutual
consent and for a time, so that you may devote yourselves
to prayer. Then come together again so that Satan will
not tempt you because of your lack of self-control."

1 CORINTHIANS 7:3-5

Eric came into the counselor's office looking troubled. He and Sylvia had just celebrated their third wedding anniversary, and he wasn't feeling good about it.

Sylvia was thrilled in her role as mother of their nine-month-old son. Eric, on the other hand, wondered whether Sylvia would ever be interested in a sex life again.

"Frankly," Eric confided to the counselor, "she treats me like I'm not important to her anymore. Since she's had the baby and been home, sex is the last thing on her mind."

Jennifer and Phil had very different backgrounds. She was

a longtime Christian; he'd become a believer shortly before they met at a singles' convention. Having led a somewhat promiscuous lifestyle in the "old days," Phil was fascinated with Jennifer's purity as well as her beauty.

Their differences didn't keep them from getting married. A few months after the wedding, though, problems became apparent. Jennifer found that Phil expected her to be sexually available most of the time—almost on demand. He couldn't understand why she wasn't as interested as he was.

Other things, like his frequent throat-clearing and occasional belching, gave her reason to be disinterested in lovemaking—especially if they'd already had sex once or twice that week. Phil felt his wife was boycotting their love life with no valid reason.

It's true that issues like these can significantly disrupt a couple's sexual expression—and a marriage, if not dealt with properly. But there's no need for Sylvia and Eric or Jennifer and Phil to panic. You don't have to, either, if you're facing a similar plight.

Here's how each of these couples dealt with their situations.

Sylvia spoke to Eric's counselor about her sexual apathy. As it turned out, fear of another pregnancy was behind her disinterest. She soon recognized that she wasn't treating Eric fairly by asking him to be "understanding" indefinitely.

Guilt feelings and "shoulds" are by no means the best

motivation for meeting your mate's needs in the bedroom. But, like Sylvia, you may have to begin there, and work on bettering your attitude. It helped Sylvia immensely just to talk to someone about her concerns. It also helped that she readily admitted Eric's needs were very important to her.

The conflicts that Jennifer and Phil had over "small irritations" had a lot to do with differing expectations about their sexual relationship. Boycotting that relationship, as Jennifer had been doing, was not the answer.

When Phil began to listen to Jennifer's concerns and hurts, it made a great deal of difference in her attitude. She became more willing to be attentive to his sexual needs, even as he became more sensitive to hers.

Not every couple struggling with sexual apathy needs to seek specialized sex therapy. Frequently having a respected pastor or Christian counselor listen and offer objective advice and support makes the difference. Often a couple realizes what has caused the apathy, but needs encouragement to face it and deal with it.

Whatever the cause of your "disappearing" sex life, don't let the situation drag on forever. Expecting a spouse to simply understand and respect the other's lack of interest isn't a long-term solution. Facing the real issues—and, if necessary, getting help—is.

—*Lon Adams*

WORTH THINKING ABOUT

Read 1 Corinthians 7:3-5 again. Practically speaking, what does it mean that spouses have a claim on one another's bodies? What challenges does that create?

WORTH PRAYING ABOUT

Praise God for His plan of two people becoming one in marriage, and ask Him to guide you as you try to make that a reality.

WORTH DOING

For the next week, leave romantic notes for your spouse in unexpected places. You might pack one in his or her lunch. You might tape one to the bathroom mirror. You might slip one in a coat pocket. Use the notes to express your gratitude, appreciation, and desire for your spouse.

Marriages aren't perfect because people aren't perfect.

I have actually heard of couples who never argue. First, I think this is extremely rare; and second, I don't think it's natural! Either they aren't being completely honest, or one of the spouses has some serious communication issues. It would be wonderful to never heatedly disagree during your married life, but that simply isn't reality. You *will* find yourself disagreeing with your mate, or being hurt by him or her. The question is: *How do we effectively communicate our grievances or differing opinions?*

The key to a healthy marriage is good communication between spouses. That includes dealing directly, openly, and fairly with conflict.

We've discovered that the success of your marriage is not based on how often you and your spouse spar; instead, it's about *how* you verbalize and express the disagreements themselves. In fact, our friends Drs. Les and Leslie Parrott, along with Dr. John Gottman, have looked at how couples "fight" and identified four negative ways of dealing with conflict. By avoiding these patterns we can more positively engage and manage disagreements with our spouse.

Here are the four common and destructive ways in which we often deal with marital conflict:

Criticism: Are we blaming our spouse rather than looking inward at ourselves?

Defensiveness: Are we allowing our pride to get in the way of honest self-evaluation?

Contempt: Are we apt to assign a negative motive to our spouse's actions rather than giving him or her the benefit of the doubt?

Stonewalling: Silence speaks its own language. Are we shutting down in the hope of making a point?

How we handle conflict is either the glue that holds us together—or the earthquake that rips us apart. In this section's devotions, you and your spouse will discover how to make sure your relationship is cohesive—not crumbling.

17

Is Fighting Fair?

*"'In your anger do not sin': Do not let the
sun go down while you are still angry,
and do not give the devil a foothold."*

EPHESIANS 4:26-27

Conflict occurs when two people have a difference of opinion that hasn't been resolved. This can happen when you and your spouse disagree over where to go for dinner or what each person's chores were this week. These are normal marital conflicts that can be worked out.

When arguments turn into verbal or physical abuse, though, it isn't healthy for any marriage. If you consistently attack your spouse with statements like, "I'm sorry I married you" or "You're so stupid," you've moved from arguing to abusing.

Throwing things at your spouse only leads to more conflict and hurt. And you *never* hit, push, shove, kick, or spit at your spouse. This is physical abuse, and it causes tremendous damage to your relationship. If this is the way you deal with conflict, you need to seek counseling to learn appropriate ways to reconcile.

Those appropriate ways don't include simply submerging

your differences instead of dealing with them honestly. Many couples try to sidestep or hide their conflict because disagreements can be painful.

Paul tries to suppress conflict because he fears fighting. "I'm afraid of divorce because of my parents," he explains. "They fought all the time and look where it led them. If Lucy and I continue to fight, I'm afraid we'll end up like them."

Contrary to what Paul believes, divorce is most common when conflict is hidden or unresolved—not when it's dealt with openly. Conflict in itself doesn't lead to divorce.

Here are 10 things to remember about resolving conflict without fighting.

1. *Deal with disagreements as soon as possible.* The longer a conflict stews, the larger the issue becomes.

2. *Be specific.* Communicate clearly what the issue is. Say something like, "It frustrates me when you don't take the trash out," rather than, "You never do what you say you will."

3. *Attack the problem, not the person.* Lashing out at your spouse leaves him or her hurt and defensive. This works against resolving conflict. Let your mate hear what the problem is from your point of view.

4. *Express feelings.* Use "I" statements to share your understanding of the conflict: "I feel hurt when you don't follow through." Avoid "you" statements like, "You're so insensitive and bossy."

5. *Stick with the subject at hand.* Don't bring two or three issues to an argument to reinforce your point. This confuses the confrontation and doesn't allow for understanding and resolution.

6. *Confront privately.* Doing so in public could embarrass your spouse. This will immediately put him or her on the defensive and shut down any desire to reconcile.

7. *Seek to understand the other person's point of view.* Try to put yourself in your spouse's shoes. That's what Mia was doing when she told her sister, "Jeff had a hard day today. His boss chewed him out. That's why he's quieter than normal, so I didn't take it personally."

8. *Set up a resolution plan.* After you've expressed your points of view and come to an understanding, share your needs and decide where to go from here.

9. *Be willing to admit when you're wrong.* Sometimes a conflict occurs because one person's behavior was inappropriate. Be willing to confess and ask forgiveness from your spouse if you've wronged her or him.

10. *Remember that maintaining the relationship is more important than winning the argument.* Finding a solution that benefits both spouses lets everybody win.

When you deal with conflict in a caring and positive way, the result can be a deeper relationship and greater intimacy.

—*Sheryl DeWitt*

WORTH THINKING ABOUT

Read Ephesians 4:26-27 again. When does anger cross the line and become sin? What can happen if the devil gets a foothold in your relationship?

WORTH PRAYING ABOUT

Ask God to give you the wisdom and self-control to channel your anger properly and express it in ways that will benefit, and not damage, your relationship.

WORTH DOING

Find a time when you and your spouse are getting along well to set some ground rules for your conflicts. Talk candidly about the tactics that hurt you or seem to make conflicts worse. Make a list of "I will" statements that you agree to honor when you argue ("I will tell you what's wrong instead of sulking or pouting" or "I will not yell at you").

18

We Can Work It Out

*"If it is possible, as far as it depends on
you, live at peace with everyone."*

ROMANS 12:18

Whether you've been married five years or five months, you've
had disagreements with your spouse. *Having* them is not the
issue. The real issue is whether you can deal with them in a
healthy way.

Each time you work out a disagreement in a healthy way,
you're better equipped to deal with the next one. Conflict handled properly can fine-tune a relationship.

Think of a lightning storm on a warm summer night.
Though the lightning itself may be scary, it helps to clean the
air. Negatively charged ions produced by the storm attach themselves to pollutants, which fall to the ground. That's why the air
smells so clean at those times.

The same is true when you deal with disagreements in an
appropriate way. Even if the discussion is loud and animated, it
can help to rid relationships of contaminants and move you in
a positive direction.

Here are some ways to deal with disagreements in your marriage.

1. *Pick the right time and place.* Get away from the telephone, TV, pager, e-mail, and other distractions. Pick a soothing, peaceful environment. Allowing 24 hours to cool down and think is also a wise strategy.

2. *Be prepared.* Understand that emotional events like birthdays, weddings, holidays, anniversaries, and graduations are a natural breeding ground for disagreements. Try to get plenty of rest before these events, and give your spouse extra grace and forgiveness.

3. *Listen more than you talk.* Seek to understand where your partner is coming from, even when you may not agree with his or her viewpoint.

4. *Keep your fingers to yourself.* Pointing fingers may be acceptable when correcting toddlers or pets, but it's not healthy between spouses. Pointing is a form of attacking, indicating that the recipient has done something terribly wrong—which often isn't the case.

5. *Keep your arguments out of the bedroom.* That's a place for unity and intimacy, not hashing out differences. Don't use sex (or lack thereof) to manipulate your partner.

6. *Remember that it's your problem, too.* If there's trouble in your relationship, it belongs to both of you! You're a vital part of a *marriage system.* When one part of the system is out of kilter,

it throws the entire system off balance. When you view your spouse's problem as your own, you're much more likely to get serious about helping to work it out.

7. *Learn to see through conflict.* Search for the real issues that often lie beneath the surface. Say, "Wait a minute. We keep arguing about all kinds of irrelevant stuff. What's the *real* problem here?"

8. *Bring God into the conversation.* Ask Him for wisdom when you can't seem to find the answers (James 1:5-6). If the two of you are Christians, nothing will put a heated argument on "pause" more quickly than two small words: "Let's pray!"

9. *Remember your vows.* Don't threaten divorce during conflict. Threats will only intensify the pain—and leave scars. "For better or worse" will not be stricken from your vows simply because you're in the middle of a major disagreement.

Are you and your spouse disagreeing? Look for mutually beneficial solutions that resolve the tension. If the conflict is too intense to handle, or if one spouse gets extremely emotional, call a time-out until you've both calmed down. If that doesn't help, involve a counselor to assist you in getting perspective.

You can't eliminate disagreements in your relationship. But by taking a proactive approach early in your marriage, you can learn to address conflict in a way that makes everyone—including the Lord—smile.

—*Mitch Temple*

WORTH THINKING ABOUT

Read Romans 12:18 again. What is the key to living in peace with your spouse? What is your role in keeping that peace?

WORTH PRAYING ABOUT

Ask God to help you understand what genuine peace can do for your relationship, and ask Him to bless your efforts to live in peace with your spouse.

WORTH DOING

Complete this sentence with your spouse: "A time I got what I wanted was when _____." Talk about the circumstances and your strategy for getting what you wanted. Would you do it again? Would that same strategy work during a conflict with your spouse? Explain.

19

Making Decisions Together

"Wives, submit to your husbands as to the Lord.... In this same way, husbands ought to love their wives as their own bodies. He who loves his wife loves himself."

EPHESIANS 5:22, 28

One of the hardest things for many couples is making a decision—especially one that satisfies both spouses.

And why not? Most corporations have difficulty in decision making. Churches have split up because they can't make a choice that pleases everybody. It's no wonder marriages struggle in this way.

Take Kathleen and Clifford. As CEO of a large company, Clifford is accustomed to calling the shots. His way of running his family, however, is taking its toll on his wife. "Cliff treats me like I'm a child or his employee," she says. "My opinion doesn't count with him. I want to do God's will, but he feels that it's the man who always gets to make the decision. I was in the corporate world before we met and made decisions that affected many people. I feel like he doesn't trust me."

If Clifford and Kathleen can figure out how to make decisions together, their marriage will be stronger. Research shows that spouses who work together to make decisions are happier and more fulfilled.

They would do well to follow the example of many couples who have learned to use each partner's strengths. If the woman is better at finances, then she's in charge of the budget. If the man is better at planning, he maps out family outings, vacations, and family devotions.

These spouses work together because they realize the goal is to make decisions in a way that's best for the family. Building on each other's strengths is the smartest thing to do.

Here are some guidelines on making decisions, which you can follow individually and together.

1. *Apply sound judgment.* God has given the two of you rational minds and the ability to investigate. He expects you to use them in your decision making.

2. *List pros and cons.* Sometimes seeing on paper the benefits and detriments of possible choices helps to put things in perspective.

3. *Consult God's Word.* When making a decision, study the Bible and see what God has to say on the subject specifically or in principle.

4. *Pray.* Many couples find that if both spouses are praying about a decision, God gives them a "peace" about taking one direction over another.

5. *Seek wise counsel.* Don't be afraid to talk to other couples, a pastor, or a mentor about your decision. Sometimes others can see more objectively than you can. This is especially helpful when the two of you have different points of view and can't seem to agree or compromise.

When most couples with a Christian commitment come to a fork in the road, they want to know their choice of direction reflects God's will. But decisions aren't always a matter of right or wrong; sometimes they're about preference. If consulting Scripture and other mature believers doesn't turn up a spiritual principle to follow, you're probably picking between two or more valid choices.

Some couples fear they'll miss the "one and only right choice," putting them "out of God's will" and dooming them to lives of misery. But God doesn't want to confuse you. As you seek Him, He promises to give you wisdom to make wise decisions.

God is waiting to give you wisdom for your next decision— both of you, working as a team.

—*Sheryl DeWitt*

WORTH THINKING ABOUT

Read Ephesians 5:22, 28 again. How can a wife submit to her husband and still be involved in decision making? If a husband loves his wife as himself, how will that affect his decision making?

WORTH PRAYING ABOUT

Ask God to help you recognize His wisdom in assigning roles to husbands and wives, and ask Him to give you a sense of peace about your respective roles.

WORTH DOING

If possible, volunteer as a couple to coach a kids' sports team. As you work together to help children learn and appreciate a sport, you may discover some helpful strategies for working together in your relationship. If sports isn't your field, try helping out in a children's class at church or leading two teams of family members to carry out service projects.

20

Agreeing to Disagree

"As iron sharpens iron, so one man sharpens another."
PROVERBS 27:17

Some couples think every difference of opinion in a marriage has to be settled. They fear disaster lurks when spouses don't agree on every issue.

Frank and Lois know better.

It's bedtime, and the two of them are once again apologizing to each other for an argument they had earlier today. They can hardly remember the subject—something about their upcoming vacation. Both were very upset and hurt by what was said, whatever it was.

A long time ago Frank and Lois made a pact to never go to bed mad, which is good. But they've wasted the better part of the day being upset over something they can barely recall—a conflict about which they could have agreed to disagree.

It's hard to guess how many arguments could be averted if couples would pray about their differences and let them go. This is hard to do, since most of us want to be "right" and justify our behavior.

Many couples, especially Christians, assume that if they're truly compatible and in love they'll agree on practically everything. They may even think that disagreement is a sign of drifting apart—or that agreeing to disagree means settling for second best.

That's a faulty judgment based on an unrealistic expectation.

Differences are usually what attract partners to one another. Agreeing to disagree, when it's appropriate, can help each of you appreciate the other's uniqueness.

If you have children, agreeing to disagree also can set a good example for them. Watching you gives them a broader perspective. Children aren't usually confused or upset by parents disagreeing, but may feel threatened by the behavior they observe when there's no resolution of a conflict.

So when should you agree to disagree? And when should you "stick to your guns"?

The answers to those questions will depend on the importance you attach to each issue. There are certain decisions such as having children, setting life goals, and choosing where to live that may require outside help to negotiate if you can't agree. Other cases—whether to have pets, where to go on vacation, how much to spend on dining out—may be easier to work out on your own. The key is your willingness to not get defensive nor to insist on "winning."

Sometimes agreeing to disagree is a choice to accept your

spouse's preference out of respect or love. For example, Dan doesn't really want to have a second child at this time. But his wife, Bonnie, does. After discussing it, Dan tells her that he won't stand in the way of her enthusiasm; he'll support and love her without resentment.

But when a disagreement can't be resolved and either of you harbors resentment that interferes with your relationship, agreeing to disagree may only be "stuffing" feelings. If that happens, get help so that the resentment can be released.

Here are some principles to keep in mind when it comes to dealing with disagreements.

1. Don't expect to agree on everything.
2. Convey your desire without anger and without having to be "right."
3. Ask yourself if you're being selfish.
4. Remember that your relationship, not the issue, is most important.
5. Try not to take things too personally.
6. Remember that building a relationship takes time.
7. Forgive, forgive, forgive.
8. Keep a sense of humor.

When disagreements arise, try using that as a checklist. Often if these principles reflect your attitude, you'll find it easier to let go of the issue you've been struggling with.

—*Romie Hurley*

WORTH THINKING ABOUT

Read Proverbs 27:17 again. If you substitute the word "spouse" for "man" in this verse, how would it apply to a marriage relationship? How does conflict sharpen us and make us better?

WORTH PRAYING ABOUT

Praise God for the variety of His creation, the fact that we are all uniquely designed, and ask Him to give you wisdom and patience as you attempt to merge your unique design with your spouse's.

WORTH DOING

Explore and embrace your differences as a couple. With your spouse, make a list of the ways the two of you are different. For example, one of you may be a morning person and the other may be a night owl. One of you may prefer classical music; the other may enjoy pop and rock. Talk about the ways you bridge those differences in your relationship by agreeing to disagree.

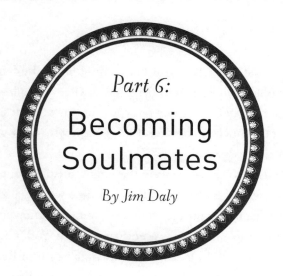

Part 6:

Becoming Soulmates

By Jim Daly

Do you believe in New Year's resolutions? If you're like many, you may have purchased a treadmill with an eye on walking more. Perhaps it was a membership at the YMCA or a health club, the purchase of a stationary bicycle, or just buying a new pair of walking shoes to encourage a regular cardiovascular routine.

Whether it's starting the routine of regular family devotions at dinner, following a personal Bible study guide, or eating less chocolate, let me commend you for setting those goals. Years ago, Jean and I started a new habit ourselves: praying together after the kids go down for the evening.

It's been a wonderful experience, not only drawing us closer together as a couple but also bonding us even more firmly to our boys.

There's something powerful and poignant about sitting

quietly while you talk and listen to the Lord as husband and wife. Problems are put into perspective when you allow yourself to simply be still in His presence. In one sense it's easy; it doesn't take much energy. Yet if it's so easy, why don't we do it more often?

We used to think we were the only Christian couple who struggled with this discipline. But over time we've realized it's a challenge felt by many other couples—even well-known pastors.

For example, during a recent trip to New York City I visited with my friend Dr. Tim Keller, senior pastor of Redeemer Presbyterian Church. Tim and his wife, Kathy, had recently penned a book on marriage and we came by their offices to talk about it.

Tim and Kathy have been married nearly forty years. When the subject of prayer came up, Kathy recalled talking with Tim one day about how they needed to get into a habit of praying more regularly as a couple.

"What if our doctor told us that we had a serious heart condition that in the past was always fatal?" Kathy asked him. "[What if] now there was a pill which, if we took it every night, would keep us alive for years and years? But you could never miss a single night, or you would die. If our doctor told us this and we believed it, we would never miss. We would never say, 'Oh, I didn't get to it.' We would do it. Right? Well, if we don't pray together every night, we are going to spiritually die."

Tim realized she was right. "The penny dropped for us

both, and we can't remember missing a night since," he said. "Even if we are far away from each other, there's always the phone. We pray very, very simply—just a couple of minutes. We pray for whatever we are most worried about as a couple, anyone or anything on our hearts that day. And we pray through the needs of our family. That's it. Simple, but so, so good."

Tim and Kathy Keller consider that decision to be a turning point in their marriage. It could also wind up being a pivotal point in *your* marriage. If you and your spouse have been reading, discussing, and praying your way through this book together, that's an excellent start. To keep your momentum going, we hope you'll consider the insights in the following section.

21

Faith Can Keep Us Together

*"Though one may be overpowered, two
can defend themselves. A cord of three
strands is not quickly broken."*

ECCLESIASTES 4:12

When Kay and Carl married, they made a commitment to honor each other. They had high moral values and a personal relationship with the Lord. Their security was in Jesus—not in themselves, not in each other.

It didn't take Kay long to realize that Carl had a lot of faults she'd failed to recognize. One was his inept handling of their money.

Kay had a choice. She could handle the problem in a way that was consistent with her faith and that took the authority of the Bible seriously, or she could turn elsewhere for advice.

She decided on an approach that echoed 1 Peter 3:3-6, which urges women to be submissive to their husbands. When Kay respectfully confronted Carl with their dilemma, he was able to hear her instead of being defensive. Now it was his turn to decide whether his response would reflect his faith.

He decided to apply principles he'd learned in 1 Timothy 3:3-6, especially the instructions to be gentle, not quarrelsome or proud or greedy. In particular, he didn't allow pride to get in the way of learning new budgeting methods.

In other words, faith helped keep them together.

Kay and Carl faced another challenge when it came to in-laws. Carl's mother had never really been excited about her only son marrying anyone—including Kay. Every family gathering was uncomfortable for Kay, and she began to feel resentful. She wanted to yell at Carl and tell him to defend her.

Instead, she prayed about the problem. She asked God to make it clear to Carl what his role as a husband should be in this situation.

Before long, Carl was choosing to follow 1 Corinthians 16:13-14: "Be on your guard; stand firm in the faith; be men of courage; be strong. Do everything in love." He took a more active part in supporting his wife, and did it in a loving way. Once again, faith helped keep these spouses together.

Then came another challenge. Carl and Kay moved to another state, leaving the church that had been an awesome support system for them. Knowing what a difference faith had made to them individually and as a couple, they looked in their new location for the nurturing and fellowship of other believers. They found it in a church with solid teaching, where they began to volunteer. Again their faith provided resources that strengthened their relationship.

Faith helps keep couples together despite the challenges of everyday life. When Carl offends Kay, for example, her understanding of what the Bible says about forgiveness is activated. So is her commitment to apply those principles. She knows that God has graciously extended forgiveness to her, and expects her to do the same for others.

Carl and Kay have pledged to be faithful to one another, which might prove difficult for Carl in his job. He works with women who are congenial and attractive. All the temptations are there—travel, creative teamwork, the opportunity to share confidences. Carl isn't blind, but the eyes of his heart are enlightened (Ephesians 1:18). Having received the gift of a relationship with God, he's not about to mess it up. He chooses to "Avoid every kind of evil" (1 Thessalonians 5:22). His commitment to Kay flows from his commitment to the Lord.

If you're a follower of Christ, staying together as a couple involves the same things that living your faith does—constantly putting aside pride, working daily on fully accepting God's forgiveness, and seeking to do what pleases Him.

—*Betty Jordan*

WORTH THINKING ABOUT

Read Ecclesiastes 4:12 again. Why is it important for God to be the third strand of your relationship? What kind of strength does He offer to married couples?

WORTH PRAYING ABOUT

Ask God to help you sense His presence and His strength in your relationship, and ask Him to help you submit to His will for your marriage.

WORTH DOING

Design and create a cord of three strands for your spouse. You can use three strings of yarn, three strips of leather, or three strands of any other material. Wind the strands around each other and then tie off the ends to create the cord. Depending on the size of the cord, you can hang it from a keychain—or perhaps from your bathroom mirror, where you'll see it every day.

22

Praying with Your Spouse

"Again, I tell you that if two of you on earth
agree about anything you ask for, it will be
done for you by my Father in heaven."

MATTHEW 18:19

A busy airline pilot, Nick found it tough to keep up with regular church attendance, personal prayer, and Bible reading. Margaret, on the other hand, was devoted to those disciplines. She wanted to pray before meals and on other occasions. The fact that praying together was so important to her made Nick feel uneasy—even irritated.

In premarital counseling, the two of them met with a mentor couple. Nick admitted that when it came to prayer, Margaret had expectations that he might not be interested in fulfilling. "I feel awkward doing that with her," he said of prayer. "Is it really better than praying by yourself?"

Deep down, Nick felt praying as a couple was something people did in "the olden days." What was the value in doing it now?

Bill and Sue also struggled with prayer. Bill had grown up in

a Christian home, watching his dad pray at the dinner table—
mainly on Sundays. At other times, his mom or a sibling would
return thanks.

Sue, meanwhile, had come from a non-Christian home.
She'd become a believer before marriage, but neither she nor
Bill had thought much about praying together.

That changed when they attended a weekend marriage
retreat. The pastor challenged all the couples to consider praying
and reading the Bible together. Sue and Bill thought it sounded
like the right thing to do, but weren't sure how to begin.

If you and your spouse are struggling with the idea of praying together, here are some things to keep in mind.

1. *Start with yourself.* A joint prayer and devotional life for a
married couple works best when it's a natural outgrowth of each
partner's personal time with God. If you haven't been praying
much yourself, you might practice on your own for a while.

2. *Don't rush it.* If you're the more interested spouse, be patient.
Praying together, like any family tradition you establish, must
emerge from what both partners agree to and feel at ease with.

In the case of Nick and Margaret, it took patience on
Margaret's part to gently nudge Nick to consider his role as a
spiritual leader. When he saw how important it was to her, he
determined to learn more about praying together and to become
more at ease with it. They began with "saying table grace," then
added other requests Margaret had shown concern for. She was
overjoyed at Nick's efforts, which in turn encouraged him.

3. *Start small.* Many couples, never having seen their parents pray together, find it an uneasy, challenging experience. Bill and Sue met the challenge by starting with what they knew.

They began by praying before meals. One day, after Sue's girlfriend at work had a miscarriage, Sue prayed about that right after Bill asked the blessing. That seemed easy enough. In time they began to kneel beside their bed at night and ask God to deal with other concerns.

4. *Use the resources available.* Can a mentoring couple or role model help you get started? Nick's Bible study friends helped him get oriented, and his pastor suggested materials he and Margaret could use. Devotional books, pamphlets, and magazines can help take the pressure off by structuring your prayer times.

These couples discovered that praying together has its benefits. Spouses were mutually inspired and helped by hearing each other's concerns and praises. They realized that praying together isn't a test to impress one another with their spirituality. After all, *God* is their audience.

—*Lon Adams*

WORTH THINKING ABOUT

Read Matthew 18:19 again. Why do you think God places such an emphasis on praying together? How can the two of you pray in a way that honors Him?

WORTH PRAYING ABOUT

Thank God for His promise to hear and answer the prayers of His committed followers, and ask Him to bless your commitment to pray together as a couple.

WORTH DOING

Create a prayer space in your house. It might be an extra bedroom, a corner of the basement, or a small area in your bedroom—anyplace that can be used specifically for prayer. Decorate the walls with quotations, Bible verses, and pictures that lend themselves to prayer. Stock it with Bibles and other prayer reference books. Create a space that's comfortable and functional for both of you.

23

Helping Your Spouse Grow Spiritually

"Therefore let us leave the elementary teachings about Christ and go on to maturity."

HEBREWS 6:1

What can you do when you and your spouse don't have the same level of spiritual maturity or interest? The answer doesn't lie in lecturing or manipulating your mate. Instead, consider the following five actions you can take to better understand your spouse and make the concept of spiritual growth more intriguing to him or her.

1. *Be patient.* Whether your spouse is a new Christian, a non-Christian, or just a nonplussed Christian, it's hard not to overreact when he or she doesn't seem to care about the most important thing in your life. But try to remember that God loves your mate even more than you do. He may be taking your partner on a journey that will ultimately produce a deeper faith.

In any event, be careful. God may *choose* to reach out to your spouse through you, but He doesn't *need* your help. Sadly, spiritual conflicts are often made worse by a spouse attempting to jump-start a mate's conscience or play the role of the Holy Spirit.

2. *Don't stand in the way.* Your behavior can attract or repel your spouse where spiritual growth is concerned. You're living out what you're experiencing with God. Is it appealing? Is your relationship with Christ making you a more enjoyable person to live with—or just a more religious one?

Those who languish spiritually especially need to see the real deal. Your mate will benefit from your companionship when you're serious about your devotion to Christ *and* realistic about your struggles, too.

3. *Be authentic.* The spouse who struggles with faith issues needs a gentle partner to come home to. A holier-than-thou approach is sure to deepen the divide—not only between your partner and yourself, but also between your partner and God (and it can't do much for your own walk with Christ, either). Nobody wants to be smothered or judged or patronized.

When you're honest about your own faith issues, you assure your spouse that it's part of the journey to have questions and doubts. Your transparency can be especially healing if your mate has felt—accurately or not—that spirituality has become a competition in your marriage.

4. *Stay balanced.* There's no doubt about the importance of faith. But it's possible to lose a healthy perspective, especially

when you feel your mate's Christian commitment is at stake. Even though you believe you can trust God with your partner's spiritual development, you may try to take matters into your own hands.

Sometimes a concerned spouse drops hints or invites others to offer unsolicited counsel to the spiritually indifferent spouse. While well intended, these approaches are manipulative. Others withdraw from a mate and become excessively involved with church or other religious endeavors.

Make no mistake: You can't be too devoted to Christ. Nor should you minimize your faith to accommodate your spouse. But over-spiritualization and hyper-religiosity will hinder your efforts as much as falling into the opposite ditch of apathy.

5. *Examine the reasons.* Before you sum up your spouse's struggle as merely a "sin issue," take some time to consider his context. What was his religious experience as a child? Was his faith nurtured or hindered? Was his parents' faith meaningful or a chore? Has he experienced a personal relationship with Christ or mere religion?

Whatever the reason, we can take comfort in the fact that God cares about our mates. The struggle may take time, and may even challenge our faith. In the meantime, we can trust Him to nurture our spouses and our marriages.

—*Rob Jackson*

WORTH THINKING ABOUT

Read Hebrews 6:1 again. What are the differences between a mature believer and an immature one? Why is continual growth important for a Christian?

WORTH PRAYING ABOUT

Ask God to help you continue to grow in your faith and assume the spiritual role in your family He has in mind for you.

WORTH DOING

Make a list of questions you have about the Christian faith. Be open and honest. If you don't understand how prayer works or why it's important, write that down. If you sometimes wrestle with questions about God's will, add them to the list as well. Share your lists with each other; then use them as the basis for a Bible study. Work together to find answers. If you're unable to answer some of them, consult your pastor.

24

Serving God as a Team

"But as for me and my household,
we will serve the LORD."

JOSHUA 24:15

"Kerri, is there any way you can help us out tonight at church? We have to have our care bags put together by tomorrow."

"Bart, I hope you're planning to be there Saturday. Mrs. Mullins needs some help moving into her apartment."

Isn't it amazing how you never run out of opportunities to serve? If you're connected to a church, there's always a need beckoning.

When your marriage is relatively new, though, it can be a challenge to balance Christian service with your relationship. Even worthy projects can deprive couples of the time they need to be alone.

Other couples struggle when one spouse is more interested than the other in Christian service. The spouse who wants to be involved may feel alone and unsupported, longing intensely for the day when both mates can serve the Lord together.

Still other couples find it hard to serve together because

their interests don't match. One may want a visible role such as performing on the drama team, while the other prefers behind-the-scenes work like setting up chairs.

How can you serve God in a way that strengthens your marriage instead of stressing it? Here are some ideas.

1. *Champion your differences.* Every talent, gift, and interest is important. God gave you and your mate varied strengths and weaknesses. Celebrate these differences and let God use them to His advantage.

Commend your spouse for his or her interest in a certain area, even if you don't share it. For example: "Beth, I really admire you for giving time to the children's ministry. I wish I had the patience you have with kids. That must be your gift."

2. *Help each other out.* Having contrasting interests, skills, and levels of enthusiasm for service doesn't mean you can't enjoy working together in each other's "specialties" from time to time.

Jason, for instance, enjoyed overseas mission trips during the summer. Val liked planning an annual couples' retreat in the fall. Was this a problem? Not necessarily.

Their solution began with sitting down at the start of the year and discussing service projects they'd like to undertake. They decided Val would serve on the retreat committee; Jason would take on added domestic chores to give Val extra time to do that. Val, in turn, would help Jason write and mail letters in the spring to gain financial backing for Jason's mission trip.

They also decided that throughout the year they'd volunteer

in a Monday night inner-city program. Jason would drive the bus; Val would teach a class.

Jason and Val are playing different roles, but supporting each other. Managing their varying interests simply calls for acceptance, imagination, and mutual give-and-take.

3. *Look for common opportunities to serve.* Ask yourself: "Are there areas of service in our church or community where we could serve God together?" Here are some ideas.

- Invite a new couple from church, or a neighbor, to come for dinner.
- Volunteer to host a movie night for the youth group in your home.
- Work in the church nursery.
- Volunteer to work at a soup kitchen or community center.
- Volunteer to transport HIV-positive kids for treatment at children's hospitals.

There are ample opportunities to serve together. Simply decide on one project together and get busy!

4. *Don't overdo it.* Feelings of closeness can be built as you serve together. Still, new marriages need "down time." This is for simply being together—talking, holding each other, serving one another, and building intimacy. As you serve together, don't let even a good thing rob you of the bonding time your relationship requires.

—*Mitch Temple*

WORTH THINKING ABOUT

Read Joshua 24:15 again. What are the biggest challenges and obstacles to serving God as a family? What specific steps can you take this week to start overcoming those obstacles?

WORTH PRAYING ABOUT

Ask God to help you honor your commitment to serve Him as a couple (or family), and to give you the wisdom and inspiration you need to overcome the obstacles in your way.

WORTH DOING

Volunteer to teach a Sunday school class together. If you've never taught before, you might want to choose a kids' class, where the lessons—and questions—can be less challenging. Work together to create an interesting learning atmosphere. If you put your heart into it, you'll find that you and your spouse will benefit from the experience as much as your students do.

Part 7:

Mastering Money

By Jean Daly

When Jim and I were first married we didn't have any money problems—because we didn't have any money.

We also didn't have any furniture. We slept on the floor for our first three years of marriage. It didn't bother us; I slept on a camping mat while in college, and Jim was also accustomed to sleeping on a mat after his year in Japan. Eventually, though, we broke down and bought some furniture.

Today Jim and I, like every other couple, still deal with financial issues.

In Western culture, we are bombarded with the message that more and newer is better. To combat the money monster, Jim and I try to talk regularly about our expenses. We are fairly typical in our finances—I tend to spend money on managing the household, and Jim tends to buy "big ticket" items. Over the years we have taken turns being responsible for paying the bills. While not always on the same page, we think we complement each other when it comes to money.

The following readings are designed to help you and your spouse dig into some of the more vexing but practical financial challenges people face in marriage. For example, how do you deal with a spouse who likes to spend while you prefer to save? How can you agree on how much to give to charity?

It's a well-known fact that disagreement over money—how it's earned, spent, saved, and invested—is the top cause of stress in marriage. Whether or not financial issues are at the top of *your* list, tough economic times are enough to make anyone's head spin. Between the fear of a pay cut or job loss, questions over how to reduce debt, or trying to invest wisely with the volatility of the stock market, it's no wonder Focus on the Family receives so many calls from families seeking both financial and relationship counseling.

We live in a culture that's constantly trying to convince us that happiness can be ours for a price. It's a lie. Yet many couples and families find themselves in debt and despair, pursuing the phantom promise that good times come when you purchase "good" things.

The Lord of the universe knows how the human heart is wired. He knows we're easily prone to wanting just a little more than we currently have—even if we have a lot. In order to help us combat these cravings God provides us with the very best available counsel to manage this challenge—the Bible.

There are over 800 references to money in the Bible, and for good reason. The love of money, wrote Paul, is the root of all kinds of evil. To confront and overcome this pull we must examine our own hearts and try to see our earthly possessions as God sees them. Working your way together through the following section will help you do just that.

25

"My Spouse Spends Too Much"

"When you ask, you do not receive, because you ask with wrong motives, that you may spend what you get on your pleasures."

JAMES 4:3

"Anna," Graham says, "we're never going to make it if you keep spending so much money."

Stress squeezes Anna's stomach. She knows Graham has been working on their finances.

"Honey, what can I do? I try not to spend too much. There are things we need."

Graham sighs. "We *need* all that lipstick? We *need* to buy new furniture and curtains for the living room?"

"Okay, the furniture and the curtains may not be needs, but my makeup—"

Graham interrupts, "Honey, you're beautiful. You don't need to spend that much on makeup."

"But I don't buy it that often." She tries to snuggle next to Graham, but he pulls away.

"You've got to take some responsibility here, Anna. Things are not okay."

As Graham and Anna have found, it can be a huge problem between husband and wife when one of them spends too much. But it's a problem the two of you can conquer together, especially if you keep the following principles in mind.

1. *Understand that you're on the same team when it comes to finances.* You can start by agreeing that you both want the same things concerning money—a certain amount of security and a certain amount of freedom. Those amounts may not be the same, but the general goals are. More importantly, you both want to emphasize the health of your relationship over the details of accounting.

When you're on the same team, it's easier to come up with creative solutions to spending disagreements. For instance, Graham and Anna might decide that each spouse will have a certain number of dollars set aside for personal supplies each month.

2. *Understand the underlying reasons why your spouse overspends.* You've probably heard a variety of reasons for overspending: deprived childhood, privileged childhood, depression, anxiety, the thrill of the hunt. All of these have one thing in common: a search for security. Consciously or not, the spender thinks something like, "If I have this, I'll be in style." Or, "I'll be accepted." Or, "I'll be okay."

Buying things doesn't provide real security. It does nothing to change God's love for us. Before making a purchase, husbands and wives need to ask themselves, "What am I trying to do?" If the answer has anything to do with finding fulfillment or escaping stress or pain, don't buy the item. It will never meet that need.

3. *Understand what things cost and how often they must be purchased.* People often enter marriage with very different experiences of spending, saving, and tithing—and preconceived ideas about what things should cost.

Marriage counselors sometimes have couples go through lists of purchases, mark down what they think the prices of those items would be, and compare notes. Something like this may be worthwhile if the two of you struggle with the costs of each other's purchases. You may also want to divide the same list into wants and needs, indicate how often you think each item should be purchased, and compare results.

4. *Understand that you must live on less than you earn.* Living from one paycheck to the next isn't comfortable for anyone. It can lead each of you to feel taken for granted, used, and insecure about the future of your marriage and finances. That insecurity is heightened when you ask the question, "What if I lost my job?"

The real problem may not be your spouse's spending or earning, but a failure to budget.

—*Sandra Lundberg*

WORTH THINKING ABOUT

Read James 4:3 again. Why is it so tempting to overspend for your own pleasure? How might a wrong attitude toward spending affect your relationship with God and your relationship with your spouse?

WORTH PRAYING ABOUT

Ask God to search your heart and show you selfish attitudes and actions that you may not be aware of, and ask Him for the wisdom and discipline to eliminate them.

WORTH DOING

Work together to create a household budget that you both understand and agree to follow. Go through your monthly bills and bank statements one at a time so you know exactly how much you're spending and putting away each month. Identify problem areas, whether it's too much spending, too little savings, or too little income, and brainstorm some solutions you can both live with.

26

How Much Should We Give?

*"Each man should give what he has decided
in his heart to give, not reluctantly or under
compulsion, for God loves a cheerful giver."*

2 CORINTHIANS 9:7

Tom and Latisha took different approaches to tithing—the practice of giving 10 percent of one's income to the church.

Tom believed they should tithe from their gross income. He backed up this idea with Bible verses on giving from the "firstfruits" (Proverbs 3:9).

Latisha didn't think believers were called to tithe in the New Testament era. She was comfortable giving when she felt like it, and thought Tom was being legalistic.

The two of them often disagreed over how to use money for tithing and other purposes. They decided to see a counselor.

The counselor started out by observing that all we have belongs to the Lord. As Psalm 24:1 puts it, "The earth is the LORD's, and everything in it." When Tom and Latisha acknowledged that, it helped them put into perspective the importance of giving back to God.

Giving is a very personal thing. Many couples struggle to decide how much money, or what portion of their income, they should give back to God. As you decide, these two principles may be helpful:

1. We are simply stewards of what God entrusts to us. When people refuse to acknowledge that, they tend to be selfish with the things God has entrusted to them.

2. The point of giving is to aid other believers, the poor, widows and orphans, and to assist in evangelism around the world (see 1 Corinthians 16:1-2; Galatians 2:10; James 1:27).

What about the question of whether you should tithe before or after taxes? Not everyone agrees on the answer. But applying the concept of firstfruits (Proverbs 3:9) would seem to recommend giving from one's total income. Following this principle would mean tithing gross income, not after taxes and Social Security and other deductions have been taken.

You may be thinking, *But we don't make enough money to give like that.* Here are some questions you may need to ask yourself.

1. What does it mean for you to be a wise steward? If you have an income, God is entrusting you with it. How does He want you to use it?

2. How have your attitudes about giving been shaped by the society around you? We live in a consumer culture, but Matthew 6 talks about storing up treasures in heaven and not

on earth. Are you caught up in a spending mentality that leaves you unable to give?

3. How might giving help you grow spiritually? Could the discipline of having less available to spend teach you something about materialism?

Even when you and your spouse have thought and talked about these questions, giving may not come easily. After all, it's contrary to the idea that possessions will give you pleasure.

So how can the two of you find joy in giving? Strangely enough, you'll find out when you begin to give. Once you see how God continues to provide for you, and how He uses what you've given, you'll probably wonder why you ever held back.

That's where Tom and Latisha ended up, though it took a while to get there. When they started tithing from their gross income and sometimes giving additional offerings, they saw that they were still able to meet their other financial responsibilities.

Latisha found herself respecting Tom's leadership in this area and beginning to share his belief in tithing from their "first-fruits." She felt more grateful for all the things God had blessed them with. When finances became tight occasionally, she even began to question whether they'd been giving faithfully.

In time, both Tom and Latisha stopped trying to blame tight finances on "imperfect" tithing. They realized that they simply needed to be good stewards in spending, saving, *and* giving.

—*Sandra Lundberg*

WORTH THINKING ABOUT

Read 2 Corinthians 9:7 again. Why is *attitude* more important than *amount* when it comes to giving? What does it mean to be a "cheerful giver"?

WORTH PRAYING ABOUT

Ask God to help you recognize just how much He's given you and to help you develop that same spirit of giving.

WORTH DOING

Ask your spouse, "When have you been happiest about giving your money, time, or a possession to someone else? When have we been happiest about giving away something as a couple?" Talk about how it felt, why it felt that way, and how you might repeat that experience this week.

27

Staying Out of Debt

"The rich rule over the poor, and the
borrower is servant to the lender."

PROVERBS 22:7

Chris and Parker had very different ways of using their credit cards. Parker used his only for emergencies, and paid them off in full at the end of the month.

Chris, on the other hand, saw credit cards as "free money." She used hers frequently, and usually didn't pay more than the minimum due.

Not surprisingly, this caused a problem. Parker feared Chris would sink them in debt. Chris thought Parker was just being a miser.

Staying out of debt isn't just a concern for "misers" like Parker. More and more couples are finding themselves "in over their heads," even bankrupt. Credit card misuse is one factor—but not the only one.

You can stay out of debt by avoiding four common pitfalls. *Pitfall #1: No budget.* Many couples never establish a budget, even though it's an excellent way to stay out of debt. Prepare your budget based on three months' expenses. Allow for savings for short-term and long-term needs. Take those savings out of your paycheck at the start of the month, not at the end of the month after spending has been done.

Once your budget reveals where you're spending your money, you can look for places to cut back as needed—making it less likely that you'll sink into red ink.

Pitfall #2: Careless credit card use. Too many couples have adopted Chris' view—that "plastic" is "free money." The result: crushing credit card debt that only gets heavier as interest is added.

Discipline yourselves not to spend what isn't in your checking account. Pay off your purchase in 30 days. Make sure credit card spending is for needs, not wants. If you've budgeted, you'll have allotted funds for needs—while wants may be beyond your means.

Pitfall #3: Unnecessary or risky loans. Budget for larger purchases, and don't buy them until you've saved the cash to pay for them.

Cars, for instance, are purchases for which many people go into debt. But cars are depreciating assets. Instead of buying the new car of your dreams, it may be best to buy a used car for which you can afford to pay cash. The same is true for other purchases that decrease in value.

The exception may be home loans. Shop carefully for a

home loan, however; terms that seem attractive in the short run may end up costing you dearly.

Pitfall #4: Ever-rising standard of living. When you get a raise, consider saving that money instead of using it to increase your standard of living. You'll have more of a "cushion" in the event of a medical crisis, layoff, or job change.

In the case of Chris and Parker, staying out of debt began with seeing a financial planner before it was too late. They avoided increased conflict and stopped the downward spiral of debt that Chris's approach threatened to put them in.

Chris learned to pay attention to her credit card balances. She also realized she was being selfish and risking their plans for financial stability. She and Parker set goals for spending and saving.

Like many people who fall into debt, Chris had felt deprived when she couldn't spend on a whim. Unlike many, however, she came to realize she'd rather wait for fewer, more durable possessions than impulsively buying a truckload of clothing and appliances that wouldn't last.

—*Sandra Lundberg*

WORTH THINKING ABOUT

Read Proverbs 22:7 again. Based on this verse, do you think God considers all lending to be a bad idea? Explain. What's the difference between a good loan and a bad loan?

WORTH PRAYING ABOUT

Ask God to give you the wisdom to create a debt-reducing financial plan that's pleasing to Him, and the discipline to carry out the plan.

WORTH DOING

Plan a credit-card-free month for your household. Make a commitment with your spouse to use only cash or debit cards for your purchases for a 30-day period. Afterward, talk about how the experiment affected your spending. See if you can come up with a modified plan for controlling your credit card use.

28

Planning for the Future

*"Go to the ant, you sluggard; consider its
ways and be wise! It has no commander, no
overseer or ruler, yet it stores its provisions in
summer and gathers its food at harvest."*

PROVERBS 6:6-8

Carly and Andrew are both 46. They haven't saved anything
for retirement yet. They've been putting kids through school,
paying the mortgage, and doing other things.

The financial planner has bad news for Carly and Andrew.
To meet their goal of retiring at age 65, they need to save a
certain amount of money every month.

The problem is, that amount is how much they make every
month—total.

Carly and Andrew will have to work longer or retire on an
income that's a lot less than what they'd assumed. Why? Because
they didn't plan early and take the steps necessary to achieve
their goals.

The longer you wait to start financial planning, the harder

it is. You limit your options for investment. And you lose the benefit of compound interest.

The further you travel down the road of marriage, the more demands there are on your income. If you have children you'll find yourself having to pay for school clothes, uniforms for extracurricular activities, maybe braces. If your parents are living, they'll be getting older, too—and may need your help. Pressures like these can make it more difficult to form the investing habit.

When it comes to long-term planning and compounding interest, every little bit counts. The sooner it's put away, the better.

The urgency to plan applies to more than retirement, too. If you have or anticipate having children, you may want to help provide for their college education. The first thing to do is establish a plan for saving and investing toward that goal.

By starting early, you can put away less money on a monthly basis to help cover the growing cost of tuition. The longer you wait, the more money you'll need to set aside each month. A financial planner can tell you about specialized programs to help fund a college education.

Some couples realize the need to start planning financially, but put it off because they don't know their way through the maze of stocks, bonds, certificates, and annuities. They need a financial planner to assist them.

Other couples need the guidance of an attorney. Have you

and your spouse prepared your wills? If you have children, have you chosen—and named in legal documents—guardians who'll care for them in the event of your death?

Few people like to think about those subjects. Many couples avoid them, claiming they'll deal with wills and guardianships "someday." But as James 4:14 says, "Why, you do not even know what will happen tomorrow. What is your life? You are a mist that appears for a little while and then vanishes."

A will determines where your assets will be directed; a medical power of attorney can outline a plan for your care if you're incapacitated and unable to tell a physician or family members what you want. Wills and guardianships are keys to a child's future; without a legal plan, children are placed under the guardianship that a court decides is best. You wouldn't want this if you were alive; why let it happen in the event of your death?

"Make plans by seeking advice," says Proverbs 20:18. And when it comes to preparing for the future, there's no time like the present.

—Sandra Lundberg

WORTH THINKING ABOUT

Read Proverbs 6:6-8 again. Besides the laziness suggested in this passage, what are some other reasons people fail to plan for the future? Which of those reasons hits closest to home in your relationship?

WORTH PRAYING ABOUT

Ask God to help you maintain a calm attitude and clearheaded view as you discuss financial planning with your spouse. Ask Him to bless your resources so that you may follow the ant's example.

WORTH DOING

Set aside some time to talk about your short-term and long-term financial goals. Be as specific as possible. Where would you like to be two years from now, as far as your finances are concerned? Where would you like to be 20 years from now?

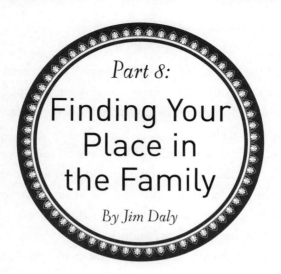

Part 8:

Finding Your Place in the Family

By Jim Daly

I know a guy who says he's number five on his wife's list of priorities—after the kids, the grandchildren, her girlfriends, and the family dog. If nothing else, he seems to know his place.

When it comes to finding our roles and respective responsibilities, Jean and I have tried to strike a better balance. We haven't always hit the mark, but we never stop trying. Through it all, we try to remember the vows we made to each other at the altar: that we would always reserve the top spot in our hearts (after the Lord, of course) for one another.

But it isn't always easy to live out. That reminds me of the story of four men who were debating which translation of the Bible was best.

The first man said he liked the *King James* because of its beautiful English. The second suggested the *New American*

Standard was closest to the original text. A third preferred the *New International Version* for its ease of understanding.

The fourth man said he preferred his parents' translation. The other three laughed.

"It's true," he explained. "They translated each page of the Bible into life. It's the most convincing translation I ever saw."

I hope our children will be able to say that someday. Meanwhile, we need to concentrate on authentically fulfilling the roles God has carved out for us in the world.

In days gone by it seemed a bit easier to know what was expected of you in a traditional family. Just a few generations ago it was common for the husband to be the breadwinner. Some wives worked before having children, but not all. And certainly by the time children came along, most women withdrew from the external workforce and devoted their lives full-time to the children.

It's important to realize, of course, that stay-at-home mothering is often an amazing blessing born of a prosperous culture and particular circumstance. Not every family is in a position to have a mother work full-time in the home. In the end, every family must decide for itself what arrangement works best for it. In fact, stay-at-home mothering, which we often call "traditional," is still a relatively new dynamic. Before the industrial revolution, families farmed together or ran small businesses. Not only didn't the father leave the home (he worked it!), the mother also assisted in the family enterprise in addition to raising the children.

But times change. For any number of reasons—including financial and cultural—many couples find themselves grappling with questions about who they are in the family and in society at large.

For example, how is it possible that two can become one (Genesis 2:24)? What does it mean to be a wife or a husband? Are there certain chores assigned to each sex—or is that an old-fashioned notion, even a byproduct of sexism?

The following readings are devoted to helping you work through some of these fundamental and critical questions as a couple. It's vital to know what the Bible has to say about the nature of husbands and wives.

Watch out for a paradox, though. If you become consumed with worrying about being your spouse's priority, you'll make yourself miserable. Don't keep score. Embrace a spirit of blessed self-forgetfulness. Instead of obsessing over what you'll get, spend your time actively loving your spouse and children—and giving everything you've got!

29

How Two Become One

"For this reason a man will leave his father
and mother and be united to his wife,
and they will become one flesh."

GENESIS 2:24

Here's a favorite that marriage therapists hear often: "If two becoming one means that I disappear as a person, forget it!"

Many couples wonder how the blending of two personalities and sets of ambitions, desires, and dreams could ever be expected by a wise and all-knowing God! Trying to adjust from "freedom" to partnership can be difficult and exasperating—but it's a process, not just a destination.

Here are two principles to remember when moving from independence to interdependence in marriage.

1. *The feelings are normal.* When we shift from being single to being married, we experience loss. Losing something leaves us feeling sad. But as we grow in our relationship with the person we committed to, the grief can turn to joy and contentment.

Nicole had waited for many years to find the right man to

spend the rest of her life with. At age 33, she met and married Ted.

Though she was certain Ted was the man God had chosen for her, Nicole missed her independence. She struggled with having to give up her "alone time" and sense of freedom.

After praying, studying the Bible, and getting direction from Christian friends, Nicole began to see that her feelings were normal. She accepted the responsibility of honoring the relationship God had given her with Ted. Though she occasionally needed time alone, Nicole learned to think in terms of two instead of one. When tempted to do her own thing at Ted's expense, she resisted. Ted responded in a similar way, and their marriage developed into a bond filled with joy and intimacy.

That's how closeness and biblical oneness develop in marriages in spite of selfish tendencies.

2. *It takes work to grow in oneness.* On a torn envelope, Sarah finds the following note left on the kitchen table one morning: "Sarah, I know you said you would like to spend time with me . . . [but] the boss called and said I have to work tonight. By the way, would you mind ironing my golf shorts when you get home? I have a tournament tomorrow."

If Sarah is like most wives, she's thinking, *How in the world does this goofball think we're going to get close if he's always gone?*

She's right; healthy relationships don't just evolve, they're nurtured.

If you find yourself struggling with the challenges of togetherness, here are some simple suggestions.

1. *Remember who brought you together.* God has united the two of you for a reason. He calls you to honor one another (Ephesians 5:22-33), to love one another (1 Corinthians 13), and to remain together until death separates you (Matthew 19:9).

2. *Change the way you think.* You're still an individual. But God has called you to leave your father and mother and unite with your spouse. That means making changes in your thinking (you belong to someone else now) as well as your behavior (you don't act like a single person anymore).

3. *Educate yourself about God's desire for unity in your marriage.* Read Bible passages that emphasize the importance of oneness and unity (John 17; 1 Corinthians 7). Personalize them by inserting your name and the name of your spouse. Pray that God will show you any attitudes and actions that stand in the way of oneness.

4. *Learn from others.* Ask couples you know who have strong marriages how they moved from independence to interdependence. What mindsets and habits did they adopt that worked for them?

They'll probably tell you that intentional intimacy is an investment that always pays off—and they'll be right.

—*Mitch Temple*

WORTH THINKING ABOUT

Read Genesis 2:24 again. In your experience, how is the "one flesh" of marriage different from the physical union of an unmarried man and woman? When you got married, did "two becoming one" seem scary, appealing, or something else?

WORTH PRAYING ABOUT

Thank God for the two things about being "one flesh" that you appreciate most.

WORTH DOING

At the next available opportunity, spend at least an hour apart from your spouse—but doing something that he or she would have liked (going to a museum, watching a sunset, reading a joke book, etc.). Then reunite. Talk about what you did or saw, and how it would have been even more enjoyable if you'd been together.

30

What Does It Mean to Be a Wife?

*"Then [the older women] can train the younger
women to love their husbands and children, to
be self-controlled and pure, to be busy at home,
to be kind, and to be subject to their husbands,
so that no one will malign the word of God."*

TITUS 2:4-5

Much of the confusion about what it means to be a wife stems from our culture's messages on the subject. Hollywood often portrays women as independent, strong, superior, and answerable to no one. Is that what a wife should be? What are her roles? What should a husband expect of her?

If you're struggling with your role (or your spouse's), you're not alone. When these issues are unresolved, it often leads to a sense of hopelessness going into the wedding and a sense of contention afterward.

Let's answer the question by looking at its opposite: What

does it *not* mean to be a wife? Here are three principles to think about.

1. *A wife is not a maid.* Some husbands expect their wives to take care of all domestic chores. Some wives are content with this arrangement, especially when the husband assumes a handyman role. But both partners should negotiate this and feel comfortable with the result.

God didn't intend a wife to be the family butler, cook, and domestic engineer without support from her husband. Just as wives are not exempt from helping out with yard work, husbands aren't excused from mutually agreed upon duties inside the home.

2. *A wife is not a doormat.* The Bible does say that the husband is the "head" of the wife, and that wives are to be in submission to their husbands. But nowhere does it grant "dictator" status to husbands, or require that wives must fulfill a husband's every wish and command, no matter how unreasonable or uncaring.

Submission is an attitude, a spirit of being under someone's leadership in the domain of marriage. Paul says in Ephesians 5:22, "Wives, submit yourselves to your husbands as to the Lord." But he also says, "Submit to one another out of reverence for Christ" (Ephesians 5:21). Submission doesn't mean that a woman can be mistreated or harmed by her husband simply because he's the leader of the home.

Submission doesn't necessarily mean agreement, either. The fact that a wife is under her husband's leadership doesn't mean she necessarily agrees with everything he does or every decision he makes.

How does that work in real life? A wife voluntarily places herself in a position of submission to God and to her husband's leadership. She doesn't give up her individuality. She gives her heart, body, and soul to a relationship of mutuality and service.

If you follow God's commands on how to treat your mate, you'll love, respect, honor, and cherish each other. You'll find no human doormats in your home.

3. *A wife is not to be the downfall of her husband.* Adam was engineered to work hard, lead his family, and overcome challenges. God gave Eve the ability, power, and free choice to either build up her husband or tear him down.

Proverbs 14:1 says, "The wise woman builds her house, but with her own hands the foolish one tears hers down." Most wives don't set out to destroy their mates. But they often allow stress, frustration, and resentment to motivate them to treat their husbands in ways that dishonor them. Constant nagging and criticism destroys a man's ability to be what he should be—a confident leader.

As Ephesians 5:33 (AMP) says, "Let the wife see that she respects and reverences her husband—that she notices him, regards him, honors him, prefers him, venerates and esteems him; and that she defers to him, praises him, and loves and admires him exceedingly."

—*Mitch Temple*

WORTH THINKING ABOUT

Read Titus 2:4-5 again. Which older men and women did you look to as role models when you got married? What did you learn from them?

WORTH PRAYING ABOUT

Thank God for the role models He put in your lives, and ask Him to mold you into the kind of spouses who will be role models for other men and women.

WORTH DOING

Write brief thank-you notes to the people who've served as role models in your lives. Tell them what you learned from them and how they've influenced your marriage, including the way you treat your spouse and the way you see yourself as a husband or wife.

31

What Does It Mean to Be a Husband?

"Now the overseer must be above reproach, the husband of but one wife, temperate, self-controlled, respectable, hospitable, able to teach, not given to drunkenness, not violent but gentle, not quarrelsome, not a lover of money."

1 TIMOTHY 3:2-3

John worked long hours at his office, providing financially for his family. That, he believed, was his duty as a husband. He didn't realize what his schedule was doing to the foundation of his family.

Before he knew it, he was living by himself.

Stunned, he asked himself why his wife had suddenly left him.

The warning signs had been there, but John had been too busy to recognize them. As a young man he'd watched his father work long hours, and came to believe that his identity and level of success depended on how others saw his accomplishments. Compliments drove his work ethic.

John was struggling with loving and accepting himself. He worked long and hard to gain the praise of others—but neglected his family because building a strong marriage usually doesn't earn many accolades.

What does it mean to be a husband? John thought he knew, but discovered otherwise.

You don't have to make the same mistake. Here are some qualities found in Ephesians 5:19-33 that help define what a husband is and does.

1. *Love shown in sacrifice and commitment.* A husband's love needs to be unselfish. It's not always tied to sexual desire, which by its nature is self-seeking.

How might things have been different for John if, when awakening every morning, he'd started the day by figuring out how to make it a special one for Susan? That act of sacrificial, committed, unselfish love could have revolutionized their relationship.

Love from a husband also needs to be natural, not dutiful. Making sacrifices out of mere duty isn't an expression of love; it may just be an effort to avoid failure and pain. That's not to say that loving deeds will always be accompanied by warm feelings; sometimes the actions come first and the feelings are a step behind.

2. *Leadership and courage.* Leaders need to first learn how to serve. Then they can lead through example. In John's case, he could have helped his family by showing how to express unconditional love, set boundaries, provide guidance, exercise self-control, and manage money.

Husbands need courage, too. But that quality isn't just about driving through thunderstorms and stopping burglars. A husband also needs the courage to admit his mistakes, and to participate in his own growing and maturing process.

3. *Sound priorities.* A husband must learn about his wife's needs, put them above his own, and respond to them—physically and emotionally. John needed to say no to his competitive drive sometimes. He needed to learn that the most rewarding thing—above applause, recognition, money, and success—is being able to love another person to the point that you would give your life for her.

4. *Communication and thanksgiving.* A husband needs to keep learning more about his wife and to communicate verbally and nonverbally. It's not healthy to trust only in yourself.

Just as a man can't read a woman's mind, a woman can't read a man's. Take time to share your thoughts. Let your spouse into your life.

5. *Unity.* Both Old and New Testaments (Genesis 2:24; Ephesians 5:31) affirm that husband and wife "will become one flesh." There's a unity that goes beyond the physical.

What does it mean to be a husband? There are many steps a man takes in his marital journey, but the first—and perhaps most important—is committing himself to fulfilling his God-ordained purpose of meeting his wife's needs.

—*Daniel Huerta*

WORTH THINKING ABOUT

Read I Timothy 3:2-3 again. Which of these qualities of a godly church overseer also apply to a godly spouse? Which quality presents the biggest challenge to you? Why?

WORTH PRAYING ABOUT

Thank God for the awesome responsibilities He's given you in your household, and ask Him for the wisdom, strength, and humility you need to honor Him in those roles.

WORTH DOING

Commit yourself to giving each other the first 15-20 minutes of your time when you get home from work. Before you do anything else, sit down or take a walk to talk about your respective days. Make your relationship your number-one priority as soon as you walk in the door.

32

Dividing Up the Chores

*"Two are better than one, because they
have a good return for their work."*

ECCLESIASTES 4:9

Now that you're married, chores are one thing you can't escape.
Your daily routine likely consists of activities like cooking meals,
doing the dishes, washing clothes, maintaining household appliances, repairing the car(s), handling the finances, parenting the
kids (if any), feeding the animals (if any), choosing insurance,
and cleaning the house or apartment.

It's common to think in terms of "male" and "female"
chores. But should a wife automatically be in charge of shower
curtains, while her husband specializes in replacing shower
heads?

Christian couples may tend to think such male/female
distinctions are biblical rather than traditional. But the Bible
doesn't specifically support the notion that, for example, only
women must cook and only men must calculate the budget
and finances. After all, Jacob prepared the stew that Esau ate

(Genesis 27); the "wife of noble character" in Proverbs 31 dealt with business concerns.

How you feel about dividing up chores has a lot to do with the way your parents handled this question.

Steve assumes the husband is supposed to handle all the chores outside the home and the wife handles those inside. That's the way his parents did things.

His wife, Abby, on the other hand, had a father who masterminded the family finances, vacuumed the floors, and did the gardening. She expects Steve to do the same.

Differences like these lead one spouse to feel the other isn't "pulling his or her weight" when it comes to household duties.

Here are some specific guidelines that may help prevent or bridge areas of conflict when it comes to chores.

1. *Think positively.* Most husbands and wives enter marriage expecting to share the load to some degree. Figuring out how to make the sharing balanced and appropriate is not only desirable, but possible.

2. *Consider the rewards.* When husband and wife work outside the home, tackling chores together lifts the load. It gives you more time for individual activities. It gives you more time together.

3. *Concentrate on giftedness, not gender.* Rather than emphasizing "male" and "female" chores, talk about which jobs you enjoy or don't mind doing. Which do you have a knack for? Which would you prefer not to do?

4. *Allow for exceptions.* Helping each other out with chores during times of stress, busyness, or illness is very much appreciated by a spouse. It also tends to be reciprocated.

5. *Write it down.* Making a list of what needs to be done is essential. It's too easy to forget who's supposed to do what.

6. *Stay flexible.* No matter how fair and equal things seem at the start, you may have to make adjustments along the way. One spouse who was at home may begin a full-time job. Another may endure serious illness or injury.

7. *Don't go strictly by the numbers.* Fair and equal doesn't necessarily mean "one for you, one for me." Remember that some chores are more difficult and time-consuming than others.

8. *Chart yours, mine, and ours.* A busy, young husband and wife struggled to balance their desire for fun with the reality of day-to-day duties. They developed a simple chart that made the "to do" list look less intimidating—and more equally distributed.

Dividing up chores is an opportunity for cooperation rather than conflict. A key to the challenge of marriage is striving to understand each other and seeking to meet each other's needs—and this is a great area in which to practice.

Even the act of discussing and dividing up what needs to be accomplished can lessen conflict. If you find yourself stuck in these issues, though, don't hesitate to seek assistance from a more experienced couple or a counselor.

—*Wilford Wooten*

WORTH THINKING ABOUT

Read Ecclesiastes 4:9 again. How well do you and your spouse work together? What steps could you take to improve your working relationship?

WORTH PRAYING ABOUT

Ask God for the wisdom to create a division of household responsibilities that's fair to you and your spouse, and ask Him to bless your work together.

WORTH DOING

Trade off your traditional chores for one week. You'll do the jobs around the house your spouse usually does, and your spouse will do your jobs. If you do it with the right attitude, you'll gain an appreciation for each other's responsibilities. You may also decide to trade certain responsibilities on a more permanent basis.

Part 9:

Having Children

By Jean Daly

Some time ago a friend e-mailed Jim and me an article from an organization called "Optimum Population Trust." The piece was titled "Children Bad for Planet."

It wasn't from the satirical Web site *The Onion* or some other fictitious entity. It was based on "research" conducted by John Guillebaud, co-chairman of OPT. He believes couples should weigh the impact of children on the planet in their family planning.

Mr. Guillebaud stated, "The greatest thing anyone . . . could do to help the future of the planet would be to have one less child." While the reporter didn't indicate what was meant by "the future of the planet," there are some who believe that humans and human activity present a threat to the survival of Earth as we know it.

It probably won't surprise you to learn that Jim and I

couldn't disagree more strongly with OPT's findings. Of course it *is* true that if *all* we're concerned about is the earth, then it is better not to have people here at all. But let's face it—that's extreme. God created the planet for us. He does want us to be good stewards of the earth, but rejecting the idea of having children is in direct contradiction to God's Word. Look how the one-child policy in China has worked out. When we start playing God, we create enormous problems.

After all, children are God's mandate! In Genesis 1:28, when God charged Adam and Eve as the representatives of mankind to "be fruitful and increase in number" and to "fill the earth," He didn't place a cap on the total. God could have said, "Once humanity reaches eight billion people, better slow things down." But He didn't.

We realize that some couples are physically unable to have children, or may have other concerns about parenthood. Seeking God's will in prayer and getting wise counsel from experts in medicine, adoption, and spiritual matters can prove very helpful.

As a matter of fact, when Jim and I started discussing our desire to have children, I was afraid of the whole thing. I feared the emotional pain that children can bring a parent. I worried that I wasn't capable of being a good mom. Jim wanted to have kids, but didn't know if the timing was right. He felt the Lord saying to him, "Jim, don't pressure Jean."

Around age 38, I had a change of heart. With the window

of childbearing closing, and having completed my college coursework in biology, I felt it was time to trust God and surrender to His will. When I went to Jim and said I was ready to start, he was excited at the chance to be a dad.

The arrival of our sons, Trent and Troy, changed our lives—and wonderfully so. Yes, there are challenging times; but what a privilege and joy it is to be entrusted with God's children. The love you feel for your children is just a foretaste of the love our Father in heaven has for us.

Whether you're preparing for the blessing of little ones, managing the challenges of toddlerhood or beyond, looking back on a lifetime of raising children, or don't plan to have kids, this section will encourage you to remember that children are indeed a gift from God.

33

Do They Really Change Everything?

*"Sons are a heritage from the LORD,
children a reward from him."*

PSALM 127:3

"I haven't slept one night in a year and a half," says a mom to a newly pregnant friend. "But I wouldn't change it for anything." She smiles and sighs wearily.

Children really do change your life.

Here are some suggestions that may help to buffer the shocks of parenthood, whether you're a longtime parent or may someday add to your family biologically or through adoption.

1. *Be prepared to adjust your assumptions.* If you've assumed that your child simply will tag along as you follow your usual schedule, you may have to think again. This may be a time in your lives when you have to give up some of your usual activities in order to provide the structure your children need.

2. *Be prepared to make sacrifices.* The truth is that you'll lose some of your freedoms if you choose to be parents. Most parents

find the joys of parenting well worth the sacrifices of redirecting time, money, and energy into their children's lives, but the costs are still quite real.

3. *Be prepared to work harder at your relationship.* You and your mate will need to adjust your expectations and be intentional about connecting. You won't know exactly how your expectations will have to change until your first child arrives. It's a sure thing, though, that if you've been dating, socializing, and hanging out for hours with friends, you'll need to adjust your timing and plan for child care. You'll still need these outlets, especially dating each other—but they will be different.

4. *Be prepared to see each other at your worst.* Since the wedding, you've probably started to see some self-centeredness in yourself and in your spouse. When the two of you are required to fill the stressful roles of parents *and* spouses 24/7/365, you'll see a lot more of these tendencies.

How can you get ready for that? Choose now to consider your spouse's needs as more important than your own (Philippians 2:3-4).

5. *Be prepared to lose sleep.* When your children are infants, they depend on you to meet every need. For some parents, that means getting up several times a night. During this stage of parenting, both of you are likely to be sleep deprived. This can hamper your ability to communicate, among other things. Watch for ways in which resulting misunderstandings can erode your relationship.

6. *Be prepared to feel conflicted.* Sometimes you'll feel torn. For example, you may have mixed emotions about leaving for work if you're employed outside the home. You won't want to leave your little one and miss the new things he or she will do today while you're gone. Yet your workplace may hold attractions of its own; it's more familiar, you don't have to sort through what your child's cries mean, and you certainly need to earn a living.

7. *Be prepared for things to get easier—eventually.* The demands of parenting change throughout a child's life span. As he or she gets older, sleeping through the night may become more common. But there will still be interruptions: calls to help a little one go to the potty, calls from a first slumber party when your child wants to come home, calls from a date that's gone awry and requires you to pick your child up.

Parenting will never be stress-free. But most parents see the challenges as well worth it. They take satisfaction in watching their children grow physically and spiritually.

—*Sandra Lundberg*

WORTH THINKING ABOUT

Read Psalm 127:3 again. Why is it important to remember that children are sent by God? If you keep that in mind, how will it affect your everyday parenting decisions—or your future parenting style?

WORTH PRAYING ABOUT

Thank God for His blessings in all seasons of your marriage, Ask Him to help you continue to give proper priority to your spouse as (or when) your family expands.

WORTH DOING

If you don't have children, set aside an evening to literally "count the cost" of having them. Make a list of ways in which your current lifestyle would change if you had a baby. After you've compiled your list, show it to friends or family members with kids so they can add items you hadn't thought of. If you already have kids, make a list of the ways your life has changed since their arrival.

34

Is It Okay Not to Have Kids?

*"So in the course of time Hannah conceived and
gave birth to a son. She named him Samuel,
saying, 'Because I asked the LORD for him.'"*

1 SAMUEL 1:20

Carson and June decided they would get their socio-economic status settled before having kids. June was a sales rep; Carson was starting his own software design company.

Their travel-filled lives didn't seem to leave any room for talking about having kids. The more successful they became, the less time they seemed to have.

On a tenth anniversary trip to South America, they finally discussed whether they would try to start a family. Both agreed that finding sitters for their house and dog was hard enough. Maybe they'd have time for kids someday—but not now.

Are Carson and June choosing wisely?

Biblically speaking, we can't ignore the fact that God considers parenthood an incredible blessing. Even more striking is

the silence of Scripture with regard to a chosen state of childlessness. It doesn't appear that the Bible ever envisioned married couples who denied themselves children. On the contrary,
Genesis 1:28 declares, "Be fruitful and increase in number; fill
the earth and subdue it."

The current tendency to ignore or dilute that command
demonstrates a rejection of God's design for humanity. From
the beginning of time, in most cases adulthood meant marriage
and marriage meant children; in most circumstances, today's
couples should carry on that pattern and look toward a future
that includes children.

Certainly there are medical conditions that prevent childbearing. Encouraging couples to have children is not meant to
imply that those who suffer the pain of infertility are less obedi-
ent to God or less valued by Him.

Some couples are convinced that kids are too expensive.
If you're just guessing that having children or expanding your
family through adoption is beyond your budget, get the facts.
A good financial planner could tell you how much it costs to
raise kids, and may be able to help you come up with a plan to
raise the money as well.

Parenting is inconvenient. Hesitations about starting a
family are understandable. The responsibilities of parenthood
can't be taken lightly, and there's no denying that children bring
major changes to your marriage and your individual lives. But

the difficulties associated with rearing children aren't reason enough to choose childlessness.

Children bring a new dimension of joy and fulfillment to a marriage that can't be found elsewhere. Parenthood ushers in a spiritual transformation that we might otherwise forego; it forces us to look outside ourselves and act sacrificially for the benefit of another.

Self-sacrifice isn't the only fear that makes couples wary of having kids, of course. Some husbands and wives, knowing their flaws or those of their own parents, are afraid they'll make a mistake that could misshape their children's lives.

No parent is perfect, and children can learn from our weaknesses as well as our strengths. If you have abusive tendencies or a family history you're afraid you'll repeat, let a counselor help you. But if you're waiting to "get your act together" 100 percent, you'll wait forever.

There are many factors involved in family planning, but the most important aspect of parenthood may be this: God gives wisdom and guidance to those who seek His help, and most parents agree that with the Lord to support them the joys of parenthood far outweigh the trials.

God is the One who ultimately gives children. Be sure to consult Him in prayer; may His blessings rest on you as you look to Him for direction.

—*Lon Adams*

WORTH THINKING ABOUT

Read 1 Samuel 1:20 again. Have you ever felt the sense of urgency Hannah felt about having a child? What can you learn from her experience?

WORTH PRAYING ABOUT

Ask God to give you a sense of peace about your current situation, and ask Him to give you the wisdom and resources you need for the next chapter of your life—whether it involves children of your own or not.

WORTH DOING

Volunteer as a couple to work in your church's nursery for a month. Spend some quality time around babies as they sleep, cry, play, and answer nature's calls. Afterward, talk openly and frankly about the experience. See if it has an impact on your thoughts about having kids of your own. If you already have children, talk about what you would say to your own kids about the joys of parenting.

35

Making Sure
Children Succeed

*"Listen, my son, to your father's instruction
and do not forsake your mother's teaching."*

PROVERBS 1:8

Most parents want their kids to succeed. But what does that mean?

For many parents, it means being the absolute best in school, athletics, language skills, and test scores. This agenda can get out of hand, causing parents to try transforming normal kids into "super kids." Unfortunately, pressing hard for excessive achievement tends to leave kids tired, stressed out, and angry.

So how should you measure success? Here are three "benchmark" questions to help you gauge healthy, God-approved success:

1. *Does the child form and nurture healthy relationships?* Strong relationships are a key to building and maintaining success. Children who don't know how to "connect" will struggle in their careers, marriages, and parenting.

Career experts say one of the skills today's employers look for most is the ability to communicate and build relationships. Even the child who absorbs incredible amounts of knowledge will struggle in the workplace if he or she isn't equipped to get along with others.

2. *Does the child know and love God and have a relationship with other Christians?* If you want your child (or a child you're close to) to be successful over the long term, show him or her how to love God and connect with His people. God designed us to love Him and to be accountable to Him as part of a community of people who do the same.

3. *Does the child have the potential to enter the marketplace as an influencer on God's behalf?* Do you want to prepare your child (or a child you're close to) to glorify God in whatever career he or she chooses and in whatever environment he or she lives?

The way you answer this question will help to determine the approach you take toward the child. As he or she learns Christlike ways to relate to others, his or her behavior will stand in stark contrast to the unhealthy, unproductive habits of the surrounding culture.

Maybe you agree with these three goals. But how do you reach them? Here are three suggestions.

1. *Model healthy relationship formation.* Demonstrate how to build productive bonds with other people. The most effective form of teaching is showing, not saying.

As the kids mature, make sure they see how you form

friendships with other adults. Allow them to observe how you interact with these adults at social events, church activities, and especially in difficult times. Let them notice how you serve your friends in their times of need.

2. *Demonstrate what it means to live your faith.* Devotional and teaching times with children are important, but they should see you praying and reading God's Word for personal benefit, too. Kids also need to witness you serving those who need help.

3. *Prepare children for positions of influence.* Teach them the why and how of godly virtues like manners, compassion, forgiveness, putting others first, seeing oneself as God does, and having patience, kindness, and love (see 2 Peter 1:5-9). Most of all, let them see you living out these virtues as you relate to them and to your spouse.

In a world that distorts success, it takes effort to stick with a healthy approach. It takes work to steer yourself away from narcissistic motivations and quests for "super kids." But it's worth discovering what God views as success, and what's best for your individual child (or a child you're close to).

—*Mitch Temple*

WORTH THINKING ABOUT

Read Proverbs 1:8 again. How much pressure do you feel to be a parent (or godparent) who has valuable insight and advice? If you don't necessarily see yourself as wise and insightful, how can you develop those qualities?

WORTH PRAYING ABOUT
Ask God to bless your efforts to become a wise and insightful parent (or uncle or aunt), and ask Him to bring role models and resources into your life to help you achieve your goals.

WORTH DOING
Make a list titled, "Things I Wish My Parents Had Taught Me." Write down the skills and information your parents neglected to pass along to you that would have been beneficial for you to learn. Think in terms of both interpersonal ("I wish I'd learned how to deal with conflict in a healthy way") and physical skills ("I wish I'd learned to be a handyman"). Discuss which of these skills you'd like to pass on to your child or a friend's child.

36

You Deserve a Break Today

*"Carry each other's burdens, and in this
way you will fulfill the law of Christ."*

GALATIANS 6:2

Having children is one of the most exciting developments in a couple's life, but can be one of the most challenging. The strain and adjustments of childrearing can cause a great deal of tension in a marriage.

It's no wonder, given the shrinking amount of time most new parents spend alone together. Quiet evenings, candlelight dinners, popcorn and a movie become almost extinct. Time to simply sit down and talk becomes a faint memory. Sex becomes a rare pleasure.

Intimacy no longer grows, it just "hangs on" if you're fortunate. Spending focused time together helps produce intimacy in marriage, and that's the very thing squeezed out by the demands of young children. If you don't make a concerted, constant effort to keep intimacy alive, your relationship will suffer.

Many couples realize that making time for each other and getting away from the kids is important—but they never seem to get around to it. Here are some thoughts that often stand in the way, along with suggestions for overcoming them.

1. *"We can't afford a babysitter, and we can't afford to go to dinner once a week."* It's easy to conclude that if you can't go out often, you may as well not go out at all. But once a month is better than never.

Look for creative ways around your tight budget. For instance, choose one night a week to get the kids in bed early, put a pizza in the oven, and enjoy an after-dinner bath together. Pick up dinner at a fast-food restaurant and head to the local park. Time together doesn't have to be expensive.

2. *"Our relatives don't live around here."* Gone are the days when most couples could rely on extended family for free child care. But there are still opportunities to go out.

Ask trusted friends at work or church to babysit your kids once in a while. Trade child care services with other parents. If faraway relatives ask what you'd like for your birthday, Christmas, or anniversary, request babysitting money.

3. *"I can't trust a babysitter with my baby; I'm afraid something will happen while I'm gone."* This is a common concern, especially for first-time mothers. It doesn't mean you're paranoid; it means you feel such a connection with your new baby that you're uncomfortable leaving him or her with someone else.

One solution is to invite the sitter to come over and watch your baby in another room while you and your husband make dinner and watch a DVD. Or, if you have (or can borrow) a cell phone, take it with you while you go out to dinner; this can go a long way in providing assurance for new parents.

4. *"Is this really worth the hassle?"* Think about the time you spent with your spouse before the baby arrived. Aim for a similar amount of "together time" in your new schedule. If you can't get anywhere close, take what you can get. The main thing is to keep a conscious, regular lookout for any and all opportunities to be a couple again.

Make sure that both of you take the initiative to plan these intimacy-building moments. Many husbands plead incompetence when it comes to "relationship stuff," but the responsibility shouldn't rest solely on the wife.

Intimacy is the lifeblood of healthy marriages. Don't let another week pass without spending time reconnecting with your spouse. A relationship starved by lack of intimacy will soon create more problems than you know what to do with, but a little planning will reap dividends for a long time.

—*Mitch Temple*

WORTH THINKING ABOUT

Read Galatians 6:2 again. How can Christian friends and family honor the spirit of this command when it comes to child care? What obstacles interfere with the practice of carrying one another's burdens?

WORTH PRAYING ABOUT

Ask God to make you burden-carriers for other parents, and ask Him to bring people into your life who will help carry your child care burdens.

WORTH DOING

If you have young children, arrange a babysitting co-op with a group of trusted friends and family members. Be careful to create an arrangement that's fair for everyone, one that doesn't take advantage of anyone and eases the burden for everyone. If you don't have young children, offer to babysit someone else's kids.

Part 10:

A Christ-centered Home

By Jean Daly

The idea of making spiritual training a centerpiece of family life isn't exactly new. After all, Moses talked about passing a heritage of faith along to the younger generation almost 4,000 years ago. Here's what he wrote:

> Impress [God's commandments] on your children. Talk about them when you sit at home and when you walk along the road, when you lie down and when you get up. Tie them as symbols on your hands and bind them on your foreheads. Write them on the doorframes of your houses and on your gates. (Deuteronomy 6:7-9)

Jim and I firmly believe that the early childhood years are prime time for laying a strong foundation of biblical truth in a child's life. A young child's perspective on the nature of God can begin to crystallize as early as age five. That's why it's so important for parents to begin giving their young ones proper spiritual training during the preschool years.

Exactly how this is to be accomplished isn't always easy to prescribe. In our family we began talking about Jesus to Trent and Troy long before they had the ability to even comprehend what we were talking about.

But there are a few principles and guidelines we recommend to parents of young children. First of all, whatever you do, keep devotional time short and simple. Children simply don't have the capacity to understand and absorb lengthy spiritual activities designed for adults. Four or five minutes devoted to one or two Bible verses, followed by a short prayer, is usually as much as preschool children can handle at any given time.

Second, where content is concerned, make good use of storytelling. A story is a powerful vehicle of communication for people of all ages, but especially for children. This includes narratives drawn from Scripture itself and stories of other kinds that illustrate biblical truths. Even if a child is too young to grasp the spiritual application at the time of its telling, a story is likely to stay with him until he's able to see its deeper meaning.

Most importantly, remember that modeling is the most effective teaching method of all. Formalized training sessions are useful, but they can never take the place of a loving parent's good example. Far more important than devotions in their impact on our children's spiritual development are the casual conversations that arise as we walk, work, or play together; the comments we make in idle moments; and the ways in which we respond to the small trials and challenges a day brings.

In the Daly house, we believe this teaching task is the most important assignment God has given us as parents. Whether you have children, grandchildren, or nieces and nephews, are you ready to accept that mission? As you explore the following section together, we hope you'll ask God how He might want you to respond.

37

Building the Foundation

"Blessed are all who fear the LORD, who
walk in his ways. . . . Your wife will be like a
fruitful vine within your house; your sons will
be like olive shoots around your table."

PSALM 128:1, 3

Many couples would like to create a "Christian home." Or
they've been told that it's important to do so. But what is a
Christian home really like? Here are some ideas.

1. *A Christian home is (mostly) happy.* If you're a Christian,
you probably agree that the source of joy is Christ. You probably
believe that when you're busy enjoying Him, your home will be
happy. But that's pretty lofty. We need some handles to really
pick up this idea.

To have a happy home, you must be "here now." You need
to be plugged in—working when you're at work, being home
when you're home. You need to pay attention to the kids when
it's time and fully experience intimacy with your spouse when
it's time.

A happy home is somewhat simplified. It's purposely *not* in chaos. The tyranny of the world and its bedlam are required to stay outside; you review regularly everything that's allowed in.

2. *A Christian home is gracious.* Home should be a safe place to mess up. Family members need the ointment of grace on the wounds of their hearts, remembering perfection is not the goal. With the world firing at you, make your home a foxhole for retreat and healing.

Grace invites humility and repentance. When a spouse or other family member wrongs you, approach that person gently. Offering grace will come back to you many times as you mess up in the future.

Gracious language says, "I expect the best of you." It avoids criticism, sarcasm, and snide humor at all times. Instead of praising only performance, it encourages, notices, and rewards effort.

3. *A Christian home is a place of service.* If you're a parent, you've tasted sacrificial service. Anyone who cleans a helpless, soiled infant or forgoes sleep to feed a hungry baby knows servanthood on a very practical level.

But why wait until parenthood? What would happen if you served your spouse from betrothal forward? Acts of kindness, respect, and self-control should flavor the Christian home. This is where husbands and wives find that serving each other in Christ is primary. Serving others is important, too—but integrity at home is foundational.

4. *A Christian home practices spiritual disciplines.* Happy families are growing spiritually. Fellowship with Christ through

the Scriptures plays a central role in a home's peace. A Christian home is where you learn how to live as you study, meditate, and pray your way through the Bible.

When you're learning to treasure Christ, He empowers you to live more simply. Your checkbook and calendar reflect your appreciation for God. Home becomes the least harried place in which you spend time.

5. *A Christian home is based on God's purposes for you.* You're probably familiar with the concept of a mission statement. This clarification of purpose is as valuable for families as it is for corporations. Developing one is a wonderful place to start crafting your Christian home. These core values and guiding principles should be flexible but consistent. They can reflect not just what you want for yourselves and your children, but also outline how you want to influence the home in which your grandchildren will be raised.

When your marriage joins with God's purposes, you get a vibrant partnership. Instead of a contrived, rule-bound facade, you discover a rich and satisfying home life.

—*Rob Jackson*

WORTH THINKING ABOUT

Read Psalm 128:1, 3 again. How does God bless families who walk in His ways? What are some of the biggest obstacles to walking in God's ways as a family?

WORTH PRAYING ABOUT

Thank God for His specific blessings on your family, and ask Him to bless your efforts to walk in His ways.

WORTH DOING

Make two lists: "What a Christian Home Is" and "What a Christian Home Isn't." Fill in as many ideas for each list as you can think of. For example, "A Christian home is a place where forgiveness can be found." Or, "A Christian home *isn't* a place where people feel uncomfortable about asking tough spiritual questions." Discuss your ideas with your spouse. Afterward, put the lists in a place where you'll see them every day. Add items to the lists as they occur to you.

38

Being a Spiritual Leader

"Wives, submit to your husbands, as is
fitting in the Lord. Husbands, love your
wives and do not be harsh with them."

Colossians 3:18-19

While the Bible clearly affirms the equality of men and women
(see Galatians 3:28), God assigned the responsibility of spiritual
leadership to husbands.

Differing roles don't mean, however, that God considers
wives inadequate, less important, or less responsible. Only an
unwise man would reject his wife's opinions and assistance, since
God created her to be his best earthly resource (see Genesis 2:18).

Where does this leave the Christian woman whose husband
is an unbeliever—or uninterested in spiritual leadership? Like
the single Christian woman, she still has a Husband who nur-
tures and equips her. Like all Christian women (and men), she
answers first to God.

The wife whose husband can't or won't be the spiritual
leader is to be an example to him and a representative of
Christ. She resists participating in anything—pornography, for

example—that would bring him spiritual harm. If he causes physical, mental, or spiritual hurt to her or their children, she carries out her duty to get them to safety immediately, lest she endanger him by enabling him to sin.

But what about husbands and wives who share an active faith in Christ? What is a spiritual leader supposed to *do*?

A spiritual servant-leader is ready to protect, help, and defend. For instance, if his wife is being treated badly by a parent, in-law, or boss, a man following Christ's example will sacrifice relational comfort when necessary to come to her defense.

A true spiritual leader imitates Christ. He's attuned to his family's needs, providing physical support, grace, and encouragement. He's concerned for the spiritual welfare of family members and takes initiative to help them grow in their relationship with God.

Even in hard times, he doesn't regard this role as boring or overly difficult. It's what he was made for. Not just willing to die for the members of his family, he's ready to live for them, too.

Since spiritual leadership grows from a man's relationship with Christ, it defies a simple description. But here are a few ideas to help you get a better picture of the qualities needed.

1. *Connection to God.* He seeks his happiness in Christ first, realizing he can lead effectively only if he has an intimate relationship with God. Understanding he has nothing to give if he doesn't first receive from God, he looks for spiritual sustenance so he'll be able to feed his family's heart.

2. *Balance.* He pursues this for the good of his faith and family. He has the freedom to enjoy his own interests, knowing it's okay to spend an occasional Saturday morning on the golf course as long as it doesn't usurp important family time. He discusses things with his wife rather than handing down unilateral decisions, finding safety in the give-and-take of their partnership.

3. *Nurture.* He attends to his family's physical health and sustenance, and considers the mental and emotional needs of each person. He seeks to superintend his family's spiritual development individually and corporately. He knows his goal is a whole, functional family, not just a bunch of polished individuals.

4. *Integrity.* He seeks to be the safest, most respected man known by his family. He deals with each person carefully, but with resolve, recognizing that he's a steward of what God has given him. His servant leadership inspires other family members to go beyond their duties and be imitators of Christ—and of him.

—*Rob Jackson*

WORTH THINKING ABOUT

Read Colossians 3:18-19 again. Why is the idea of submission in marriage challenging? What specific steps can you take to make it less challenging in your relationship?

WORTH PRAYING ABOUT

Ask God to give you a sense of peace about your role in your family, and ask Him to give you the wisdom and confidence to embrace that role, according to His will.

WORTH DOING

Plan a literal "leading" exercise for the husband to conduct. He should come up with an excursion, perhaps a nature hike or a trek through the city, in which he leads the way. The wife (and kids, if present) may offer input along the way, but ultimately it's the husband who decides where to go. Afterward, compare the literal exercise with the challenges of being a leader and being a submitter in your marital relationship.

39

When You Like
Different Churches

*"Let us not give up meeting together, as some are in
the habit of doing, but let us encourage one another—
and all the more as you see the Day approaching."*

<small>HEBREWS 10:25</small>

Jim and Janet met at a large "seeker" church. They were happy
with the casual services and the charismatic emphasis.

One day, Jim was invited by a Christian co-worker to a
vesper service at an Eastern Orthodox congregation. Both Jim
and Janet found it totally unfamiliar; people stood most of the
time, didn't make expressive gestures, used incense and icons,
and followed a formal, liturgical order of service.

Jim found himself attracted to this different form of worship. Janet was completely turned off and wanted nothing further to do with it.

After considerable struggle over the issue, Jim continued to
attend the Orthodox church. Janet often accompanied him, but

didn't share his passion for the experience. In consideration of her feelings and needs, Jim sometimes chose to go with her to a church in which she felt more at home.

This compromise wasn't totally satisfying to either. But it did keep them together for worship.

The dilemma of Jim and Janet suggests a few principles you might want to consider—especially if you and your spouse are having trouble in this area.

1. *Husbands have a spiritual leadership role—within limits.* Whenever possible, the wife is to respect and follow that leadership rather than openly rebelling against it or passively undercutting her spouse's efforts. The husband also is to love his wife "as Christ loved the church and gave himself up for her" (Ephesians 5:25). He has a sacred duty not to trample on or ignore his wife's needs, preferences, and feelings.

If a husband is "leading" his wife and family into churches or practices that are heretical or cultic, of course, the wife has to put her spiritual foot down and refuse to participate. Her first allegiance is to God and His truth. Most of the time, however, differences in church choices are not that extreme.

2. *Give your relationship priority.* God doesn't want a dispute over church choice to tear your marriage apart. Try to compromise in a way that both of you can live with. Perhaps you've considered only a few churches, and there are more you can visit. Keep looking for a place of worship that provides for the

spiritual growth of both spouses—and your children, if you have any.

3. *Try creative alternatives.* Many churches provide both "traditional" and "contemporary" services. Some couples attend a Saturday night "contemporary" meeting but also occasionally a Sunday morning "traditional" service at the same church.

Some spouses attend completely different churches. This is rarely a positive, long-term solution, however; it separates partners rather than engaging them together in a marriage-enriching, spiritual experience.

Some husbands and wives decide to "solve" the problem by skipping church altogether. Clearly this is not a decision God would want for them; Scripture states that Christians are not to abandon fellowship with other believers (Hebrews 10:25).

If you're at an impasse on this issue, don't despair. Keep praying with each other that God will give you a solution. Examine your own motives, asking yourself why you find it so hard to accommodate your spouse. You may discover that this argument is a symptom of deeper problems in your relationship—control needs, conflict management, or plain old selfishness. Address these issues—in Christian marriage counseling, if necessary.

Most couples, if they're seeking to please God and not just themselves, do eventually find a church where both spouses are satisfied. You can, too.

—*Phillip J. Swihart*

WORTH THINKING ABOUT

Read Hebrews 10:25 again. Why does God place such importance on regular Christian fellowship? What are some of the biggest obstacles to maintaining a regular church presence?

WORTH PRAYING ABOUT

Thank God for His gift of fellowship, the support of other believers, and ask Him to guide your discussions with your spouse about where you will worship.

WORTH DOING

Design a "bulletin"—an order of worship brochure—for your ideal church service. Your spouse should do the same. The bulletin should reflect your worship preferences. How much formality do you prefer? What kind of music do you like? How many drama and performance elements should there be? What's a meaningful sermon topic? Be as specific as possible in designing your bulletin. Afterward, compare your results with your spouse's.

40

Helping Kids Grow Spiritually

"These commandments that I give you today are to be upon your hearts. Impress them on your children. Talk about them when you sit at home and when you walk along the road, when you lie down and when you get up. Tie them as symbols on your hands and bind them on your foreheads. Write them on the doorframes of your houses and on your gates."

Deuteronomy 6:6-9

Most Christian parents probably would agree that the spiritual training of their children is important, but feel they don't have the time, energy, or qualifications. They might be surprised to know that spiritual training isn't as hard as they think.

Here are some practical ways to develop your child's spiritual life.

1. *Family devotions or family nights.* Make family devotions brief and age-appropriate. Deal with issues your child might be dealing with. If you have a preschooler, try reading or acting out

Bible stories; if you have a teenager, discuss issues like peer pressure and how to wisely choose friends, referring to verses like, "Do not be misled: 'Bad company corrupts good character'" (1 Corinthians 15:33). Help kids see that Scripture is applicable and necessary to daily living.

Family nights are a less traditional way to accomplish similar goals. These fun times with a spiritual point might feature anything from games to object lessons to watching and discussing a movie.

2. *Prayer time.* Pray with your child about personal struggles—finding friends, passing a test, performing in a sporting event. When God answers a prayer, call it to your child's attention and thank the Lord for what He's done. In this way you teach your child to ask God about life decisions because He's interested in your child and wants to be close to him or her.

3. *Teachable moments.* Use everyday events to teach your children biblical principles. Teachable moments can come at any time. They needn't be structured; casual is fine. You might tell the story of Noah as you drive through the rain, for example, or talk about revenge when you pass a billboard advertising a violent movie.

4. *Church and youth group.* Spending time with other Christian kids can boost your child's spiritual growth. Worship services and youth group activities should reinforce what your child is being taught at home—and allow your child to develop friendships with peers who share your family's values and beliefs.

5. *Mission trips.* These are opportunities for fellowship and for practicing some of the biblical principles your child is learning at home. They're also a powerful way to show kids how the rest of the world lives.

6. *Parental modeling.* Most important for children's spiritual training is seeing active faith modeled in their parents' lives. If you're not demonstrating the value of a relationship with God, your children won't buy it. No one expects you to be perfect, but your actions truly speak louder than your words.

What if your spouse won't take an active role in spiritually training your child? This is a problem for many couples.

It's good to encourage each other to train your children. But don't nag your spouse about it or confront him or her in front of the kids. Do the training yourself if needed, praying for your mate to help. If your spouse keeps resisting, just keep living your faith and teaching your children.

Whether you go it alone or work as a team, giving your child a strong spiritual heritage is the best way to equip him or her to face the challenges ahead.

—*Sheryl DeWitt*

WORTH THINKING ABOUT

Read Deuteronomy 6:6-9 again. How can you make discussions about God's work and will a normal part of your family life (or your interaction with kids)? What are some alternatives to writing His commandments on the doorframes of your house?

WORTH PRAYING ABOUT

Ask God for the wisdom and strength to meet the awesome challenge of spiritually nurturing your kids (or young relatives), and ask Him for the resources to do it according to His will.

WORTH DOING

Plan a performance of a Bible story with your spouse and kids. If you don't have kids, recruit some from your friends, your church, or your neighbors. Choose a story, assign roles, and spend some time practicing. When you're ready, invite people to your performance.

Part 11:

Emotions in Motion

By Jim Daly

In the following pages you're going to read about challenging bumps along life's marital road: keeping the romance alive, handling rational (or irrational) feelings, and dealing with the irritating habits of a spouse. These topics have one thing in common: strong emotions.

Many years ago Dr. James Dobson, Focus on the Family's founder and my longtime boss, wrote an entire book predicated on one question, which was also the title of the project: *Emotions: Can You Trust Them?*

The simple answer is "No." Our emotions are like the tides of the sea—they ebb and flow and come in and go out.

When I was a teenager, I sat in world history class dreaming of football when the teacher started talking about a weather condition known as "the doldrums." The doldrums occur when the prevailing winds stop blowing and an extended calm settles on the open sea. That's a serious problem if you're a sailor relying on wind power to get where you're going.

Thousands of years ago, European sailors on a quest to reach new lands would sometimes encounter the doldrums during a voyage across the equatorial region of the Atlantic Ocean. Trapped in this peculiar weather pattern for weeks— even months—on end, they could run out of rations and fresh water. Even the most seasoned sailor might experience cabin fever or death.

Let's face it. Every couple sometimes inadvertently sails into the relational doldrums—a season when things have stagnated in the marriage. Signs of the doldrums might be that you've stopped having regular dates, you find you rarely have something new or interesting to talk about so your conversation becomes perfunctory, or you maintain different schedules and are nothing more than ships passing in the night.

Remaining in the doldrums is deadly for a sailor. Likewise, it can be deadly for your marriage to drift along without encountering a fresh burst of wind in your sails. If you find yourselves in just such a predicament—or want to avoid one—these next words are especially for you.

41

Let's Talk About Feelings

*"Finally, all of you, live in harmony with one another;
be sympathetic . . . be compassionate and humble."*

1 PETER 3:8

Janeen is having trouble with a co-worker. Her husband, Jerry, listens to her story for a while, then proceeds to tell Janeen what she should do. For Jerry the subject is closed; the problem is solved.

But Janeen doesn't want a problem-solving session. She only desires to be heard. She needs Jerry to be a safe sounding board.

Even though this discussion didn't begin with an issue between Janeen and Jerry, it ends there. Janeen's response is resentment and bitterness. Next time she needs to talk about feelings, she may not confide in him.

A week later Jerry has a disagreement with his father. Janeen, wanting to be helpful, follows Jerry around and tries to get him to talk about his feelings. But Jerry needs to be by himself to give this situation some thought.

Jerry, like most men, needs space to work through problems. Not understanding this, Janeen triggers an argument. Next time Jerry may not reveal his pain to her, either.

Whether you're more like Janeen or Jerry, you want a partner who honors you by listening when you're ready. You want your spouse to acknowledge your pain, to hear the options you've formulated, to give you equal status.

Intimacy in a marriage begins when each spouse takes responsibility for his or her emotions and behaviors. This is more likely to happen in a climate free from judgment, defensiveness, and blame.

When Janeen reports problems with a co-worker and Jerry responds as problem solver, she can use "straight talk" with him. For example: "When I'm not allowed to finish my sentences, I feel discounted and unimportant to you. What I need is to be heard."

When Jerry takes responsibility for the hurt he feels because of his father's comments, Janeen can promote intimacy by listening. She can draw him out to express what he's ready to say. Only when Jerry feels safe will he disclose to Janeen his deepest feelings and any related history. Their closeness will be enhanced.

When you have feelings you'd like to express, it may be helpful to pray or journal about them first. Tell your heavenly Father how you're feeling before you address the issue with your mate.

Talking about feelings is challenging enough in itself, but other factors can make it harder. First, there's the "child challenge." If you have kids, they're probably clamoring for attention when the two of you need time to talk. Janeen and Jerry, who have eight-month-old twin boys, need to develop intimacy skills and schedule time to address feelings.

Then there's the "childhood challenge." Sometimes a person enters a marriage without having been nurtured as a child. Missy, for example, had a mother who was an alcoholic. Never experiencing unconditional love, Missy became the "parent" at age three. When her husband, William, attempts to nurture her now by talking about feelings—even positive ones like love, joy, and peace—it feels foreign and uncomfortable to her. Missy and William may need counseling to address this unfinished business, so she can express feelings and receive nurturing.

So how can you talk about feelings?

- By being respectful and honoring when your spouse takes responsibility for his or her emotions and behaviors;
- By understanding how the communication styles of men and women differ;
- By developing conflict resolution strategies;
- By intentionally nurturing one another;
- By committing yourself to creating an enjoyable marriage; and
- By keeping a prayer journal to release frustration.

This sets the stage for safe self-disclosure. What happens next is up to you.

—*Betty Jordan*

WORTH THINKING ABOUT

Read 1 Peter 3:8 again. How do these instructions to all believers apply specifically to Christian spouses? Why are harmony, sympathy, compassion, and humility important in responding to your spouse's feelings?

WORTH PRAYING ABOUT

Ask God to give you a heart that's sensitive to your spouse's emotional needs, and the wisdom to respond to them in a helpful, loving way.

WORTH DOING

Write several feelings-related words on index cards, one word per card. Use expected words like "Frustrated," "Nervous," "Loved," and "Energized," as well as some unexpected ones, like "Trapped," "Confused," "Relaxed," and "Sexy." Each day for a week—once in the morning and once in the evening—you and your spouse will choose a card that reflects your feelings at that particular moment. Briefly discuss your choices and explain why you chose them.

42

Those Irritating Habits

"Finally, brothers, whatever is true, whatever
is noble, whatever is right, whatever is
pure, whatever is lovely, whatever is
admirable—if anything is excellent or
praiseworthy—think about such things."

PHILIPPIANS 4:8

"Cathy is always late for everything. Last week I decided to go on to church without her, and then for some reason she gets mad at me!"

"Bob thinks it's funny to start burping contests at the table with our boys. It is *very* embarrassing."

Do you have to live with these habits? Should loving this person be enough to enable you to overlook them? And if you can't, should you feel guilty?

Being annoyed by your spouse's habits is normal. The key is to learn to work together to change the habits that can be changed and learn to accept those that can't.

First, ask yourself why you want your spouse to change. Is

it for your own good only? If changing the habit would truly benefit both of you, change may be worth trying. But keep these guidelines in mind:

1. *Address the problem honestly.* "Honey, it bothers me when you burp at the table. It teaches the children a bad habit."

2. *Explain the benefit of change.* "Eating at the table will be more pleasant for all of us."

3. *Don't command change.* "You're such a slob at the table. Stop being so messy." Instead, *request* change. Your spouse will respond more favorably.

4. *Don't attack your mate.* "You are a horrible listener. It's no wonder no one talks to you." Confront the problem; don't attack the person.

5. *Discuss ways to bring about change.* Let your spouse know that you're on his or her side. Help him or her find ways to change those habit patterns. If the problem is overeating, for instance, go with your spouse to the gym, cook healthy meals, and go out to eat less often.

6. *Encourage your spouse's growth.* "You're doing a great job. I'm really proud of the effort I see. Thank you for your dedication to making this change."

7. *Recognize that change takes time.* Be patient with your spouse. Praise little steps that you see.

8. *Focus on your spouse's good habits, not just the irritating ones.* One wife whose husband always left a ring in the bathtub

found her perspective changing when her husband was in an accident. "When John came home several days later, I found myself sitting in the bathroom and thanking the Lord that I would have more time with John and more rings in the tub. I was reminded of Philippians 4:8. . . . When I see the ring now, I turn my thoughts to the wonderful qualities of my husband and the annoyance of that ring in the tub disappears."

9. *Pray for your spouse.* God is ultimately the one who makes change possible in any of us. And since some behaviors may never change, ask God to give you grace to accept the differences between you and your spouse.

10. *Seek to change the habit, not the person.* It's possible to help your spouse drop an irritating habit—as long as it's the habit you're trying to change. If you're trying to alter your spouse's personality, you'll be fighting a losing battle that will end in frustration for both of you.

If you follow the aforementioned guidelines and don't meet with success, it's time to ask yourself whether the battle is worth it. Some habits are so engrained that if they don't involve moral issues or character flaws, it may be best to live with them.

Keep praying for your spouse. And when you think of him or her, focus on his or her positive traits—instead of that irritating habit.

—*Sheryl DeWitt*

WORTH THINKING ABOUT

Read Philippians 4:8 again. How did this work for John's wife? What, other than a serious accident involving your spouse, would motivate you to try this way of dealing with irritating habits?

WORTH PRAYING ABOUT

Like John's wife, thank God that the two of you have each other—even if it means putting up with bathtub rings, being late, or burping contests at the table.

WORTH DOING

If you can, watch a television show or movie about a married couple. How does the couple deal with irritating habits? Are the results funny or depressing? How does the approach of these spouses compare with a strategy based on Philippians 4:8?

43

Keeping Romance Alive

"My lover is mine and I am his."
SONG OF SONGS 2:16

Megan says she and her husband, Terry, have lost the romance in their marriage. They have two children, and Megan spends every waking hour caring for the needs of her family. At the end of the day she's exhausted, with no energy for candlelight dinners.

What should Megan and Terry do? Is there a list of "rules for romance" they need to follow?

Not exactly. It's actually a deeper issue; the presence of romance reflects the overall quality of a maturing relationship.

A man who was one of four sons tells how, every night, his father would come home and walk right past his boys. He would go directly to his wife and give her a hug and a kiss. Then he would turn to the four little stairsteps who were watching, and say, "I think I am falling in love with your mom."

That man—and his sons—knew something about how romance can survive in a marriage.

So what can you do to help romance survive in yours?

1. *Recall your beginnings.* Remember when you first met and fell in love. What characterized your relationship? Did you listen to every word your intended said?

You probably were considerate and filled with respect. Each of you gave the other your complete, constant attention. You overlooked each other's faults and wanted to be together.

Was your love based on reality? Not the "reality" of annoying habits and thoughtless slights you may have catalogued since the honeymoon. But aren't the qualities that attracted you to each other just as real? Maybe it's time to rediscover them.

2. *Give up the spotlight.* Now that Megan and Terry have children, Megan can't give all her attention to Terry. Terry can't do that for Megan, either; he may be focusing on his work or a home project to make life better for his family.

Part of maturity is not needing to be the center of attention. Both Megan and Terry can demonstrate love for each other, but in new ways—indirectly as well as directly. As long as each of them views the other's role with respect and consideration, romance—idealized love—doesn't have to elude them.

3. *Live under God's authority.* Keeping romance alive is a lot easier when you're growing the fruit of the Spirit—love, joy, peace, patience, kindness, goodness (love in action), faithfulness, gentleness, and self-control (Galatians 5:22-23). When Megan and Terry submit to God, the spark of romance not only has a chance of being rekindled, but can become a radiant flame.

4. *Honor each other*. In their book *It Takes Two to Tango*, Gary and Norma Smalley offer this advice on honoring your spouse: "When you honor your wife, she will sense that nothing and no one in the world is more important to you. She won't have to wonder if she's number one—she'll know." The same goes for a wife's treatment of her husband.

5. *Be honest*. If you and your mate feel you can't be honest with each other, let a Christian counselor or pastor help get the conversation going.

Keeping romance alive requires effort and creativity. It means honoring one another by being honest, kind, and respectful in your responses, showing affection throughout the day without expecting sexual intimacy, having a regular date night, lighting candles or having a sweet fragrance in the bedroom, praying together, sharing feelings, and taking responsibility for your offenses.

Romance is a living, growing love. Things that grow require "tending to." No one can do this alone. It takes both marriage partners giving their all; it takes reliance on the Holy Spirit to empower you, especially in the darkest hours.

—*Betty Jordan*

WORTH THINKING ABOUT

Read Song of Songs 2:16 again. What are the best things about having someone in this world who is yours? Why do we sometimes forget what a blessing that is?

WORTH PRAYING ABOUT

Thank God for bringing your spouse into your life, and ask Him to bless your efforts to keep your romance alive.

WORTH DOING

Make a romantic "mix CD" or iPod playlist for your spouse. Include certain songs that have personal meaning for the two of you and other songs that convey your feelings for your spouse. Play your playlists for each other during a romantic night at home.

44

Should We Settle for Less?

"And my God will meet all your needs according
to his glorious riches in Christ Jesus."

PHILIPPIANS 4:19

Martha's dad was a real "fix-it" guy. But when Martha married her husband, Chuck, she was shocked to discover that he was nothing like her dad. Chuck had no problem ignoring an ever-growing list of things around their house that needed tightening, replacement, or repair.

Chuck had never been handy with home repairs, since he and his single mother lived in an apartment. Chuck's mom usually just notified the landlord when something needed attention.

When it came to fixing things, Martha had to settle for less. Should a spouse have to do that?

What we usually mean when we ask, "Do I have to settle for less?" is "Do I have to settle for less than I expected?"

Let's rethink the whole issue by asking, "Does my disappointment have to do with something my spouse could change? Is my dissatisfaction based on comparison? How does all of this square with my wedding vows? Didn't I say something like, 'forsaking all others' and 'for better or worse'?"

There are three ways *not* to deal with the question of settling for less: being self-centered, growing cynical, and seeking revenge. Instead, try asking, "Is there anything my spouse can do to improve this situation? Does he or she understand how important it is to me? Have we talked and prayed about it?" Your job may be to love and accept the one you've chosen, and trust God to motivate change according to His plan.

In Martha's case, she finally realized she loved Chuck for all the positive things he represented—not for what he couldn't (or hadn't yet learned to) do in the way of home repair. It was a tough lesson, but accepting Chuck's limitations was part of Martha's maturation process.

You can also choose to defuse cynicism by maintaining a sense of humor. Martha may shrug and say, "Boy, is my dad going to be glad about all the stuff he gets to fix at our house!"

Jerry was a man who struggled with settling for less. He'd always wanted to marry a woman who'd "saved herself" for him. But then he'd met Lucy, a divorced single mom, at a church picnic. He'd been struck with Lucy's strong spiritual character, and was immediately accepted by Lucy's daughter, Heather.

When Jerry allowed himself to think about the idea of marrying Lucy, he found himself in conflict. If he married her, he'd have to accept that she'd been another man's wife.

The more Jerry—with a pastor's help—grappled with his feelings about Lucy's past, the more he realized Lucy couldn't change it. He'd either have to accept and forgive it, or move on without her.

Jerry decided that having Lucy and Heather in his life was more important than the feeling that he'd have to settle for less. His disappointment was finally resolved when he and Lucy made a commitment to each other.

Are you struggling with "settling"? Here are five things to remember.

1. You aren't alone. God, who loves you, knows about your situation. He wants more for you than you could ever imagine (see Ephesians 3:20).
2. Accepting your mate as he or she really is demonstrates your growth in maturity and love. That goes hand in hand with forgiving his or her shortcomings.
3. If you respectfully discuss your unmet expectations with your spouse, change may be possible. If it isn't, forgiveness is the salve that comforts those unfulfilled hopes.
4. This is a two-way street. Consider whether your spouse is already accepting and forgiving some trait of yours that he or she would prefer to see changed.
5. Discussing these issues in the presence of a third party, such as a pastor or therapist, can help.

—*Lon Adams*

WORTH THINKING ABOUT

Read Philippians 4:19 again. To understand how this verse might apply to marriage, why is it important to know the difference between "needs" and "wants"?

WORTH PRAYING ABOUT

Thank God for a specific way in which you've seen Him meet a need in your marriage—financial, spiritual, emotional, or physical.

WORTH DOING

"[Jerry's] disappointment was finally resolved when he and Lucy made a commitment to each other." Plan and carry out a "commitment celebration"—anything from exchanging paper rings to a full-scale party—declaring your loyalty to each other despite the fact that your marriage is still a work in progress.

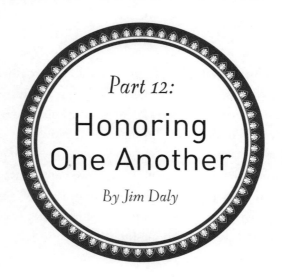

Part 12:

Honoring
One Another

By Jim Daly

What does it mean to honor your spouse? Does it just mean avoiding adultery?

It would be easy to look toward the seventh commandment as a way to measure whether we're "honoring" our spouse by remaining faithful and exclusive. But in the context of a lifelong relationship, honoring one another extends well beyond that.

As I think about how Jean and I have tried to "honor" one another throughout nearly three decades of marriage, I'd have to say that our habits have been relatively simple. For example, we've always tried to consult one another when it comes to major decisions—whether it's buying a house or accepting a promotion at work. We honor each other with our conversation—both to each other and how we speak of the other to our family, friends, and neighbors.

As I've previously shared, my parents didn't have a great

marriage. Far from it. In short, my mom decided to divorce my dad when I was almost five years old due to his unshakeable addiction to alcohol. Dad wasn't the least bit happy about the news that Mom was going through with the divorce.

One night while Mom was at work and my siblings and I were home watching television, Dad showed up. He was drunk and armed with a ball-peen hammer and a jug of burgundy wine. The fiery look in his eyes and the threats he spewed made it clear he had every intention of hurting my mother.

Staggering through the house looking for her, yet not finding her, Dad roared, "This is what I'm going to do to your mother!"

Boom! He plowed the hammer into the wall, blasting a giant hole where metal met drywall. The force of the blow seemed to rattle our house to the foundation—not to mention the damage it did to the five of us young kids who were praying we weren't his next target.

Not surprisingly, there is a drastically different dynamic in our own house these days. By no means are Jean and I perfect, but there is a sweet aroma in the air of the home where spouses respect one another.

Regardless of how you may feel about your relationship at the moment, try to step back and ask yourself how the Lord sees your spouse and your marriage. We believe that when you learn to see your marriage through the eyes of God, you'll discover the divine purpose He had in mind when He brought you and your spouse together. The following devotions can help the two of you take that kind of fresh look at your journey.

In turn, you can experience deeper affection, better communication, and a rekindling of the romance you once shared. If that sounds worthwhile—and even enjoyable—it is!

45

Trying to Change Your Spouse?

"And he said: 'I tell you the truth, unless you change and become like little children, you will never enter the kingdom of heaven."

MATTHEW 18:3

A psychologist named Dr. Negri once decided his fiancée needed to change. Figuring he'd get an early start, he set out to remake the woman before they married. In therapy sessions he attempted to mold his patient, 30 years younger, into the perfect spouse.

After treatment was completed, they married. But the therapy seemed to fail as soon as he got the wedding ring on her finger.

She didn't want to wash the dishes or vacuum. Dr. Negri often had to watch their baby because his wife refused. The couple ended up in divorce court.

The psychologist said that he made one mistake when he took on the transformation. He forgot to do therapy on himself.

By now you may have noticed certain "flaws" in your spouse. Maybe you've tried for a long time to get your spouse to change. But it hasn't worked.

There are primarily two reasons why you might want to change your spouse.

1. *You want to see your spouse replicate your actions.* If you squeeze the toothpaste from the bottom of the tube, or put the toilet seat cover down, you probably want your spouse to do so, too. It's easy to approach differences with the attitude that your way is the right way.

2. *You want your spouse to meet your needs.* The more needy you are, the more likely you have a detailed agenda of what you want those changes to look like.

Which of these reasons applies to you?

Maybe you want your spouse to be like you. But consider the truth that God wants you and your unique qualities to work with your spouse's unique characteristics. Instead of trying to make your mate "see things your way," you can benefit from having different perspectives. If you and your spouse view a situation from slightly different vantage points, you can blend those views and see things more accurately than either of you could individually.

Do you want your spouse to change in order to meet your needs? It's not unreasonable to want your needs met. But in Philippians 2:4 Paul says, "Each of you should look not only to your own interests, but also to the interests of others." Are you as concerned about responding to your spouse's interests as you are with how your interests can be served?

There's nothing wrong with wanting to see your spouse change and grow. But you can only change *you*!

That doesn't mean there are no limits to what's appropriate in a marriage. You don't need to accept abusive behavior. Physical aggression toward a spouse is never right. Name-calling and belittling words also violate the God-given value to be reflected toward a mate.

What if you want change for reasons that aren't selfish?

If you have a concern, take ownership of your feelings. Voice them honestly and respectfully. Sometimes expressing them in a note can reduce defensiveness and cut through communication difficulties.

Consider the case of Bill and Sue.

For the first few years of their marriage, Bill saw their differences as a threat to his "headship." He tried unsuccessfully to "get her in line."

Finally Bill realized that his job was not to change Sue. He tried voicing his concerns constructively to her: "I know that there's been a lot going on for you lately, but I feel frustrated when clothes are left lying around the apartment. Is it something I can help you with?"

When Bill gave Sue the freedom to see issues from her

viewpoint, he found that in the areas that mattered most she was willing to make adjustments. He also realized that many changes he'd thought necessary were not.

—*Glenn Lutjens*

WORTH THINKING ABOUT

Read Matthew 18:3 again. If spouses can't expect to change each other, why did Jesus call people to change? How could becoming more like a child help a marriage?

WORTH PRAYING ABOUT

Ask God to help each of you tell the difference between changes in your marriage that are necessary and those that aren't.

WORTH DOING

Write your spouse a note about a *small* change you'd like to see in your relationship, your division of household chores, or your schedule. Voice your feelings and suggestions honestly and respectfully. Give each other a week to think and pray about what God would like you to do as a result.

46

Forgiving Each Other

*"And when you stand praying, if you hold
anything against anyone, forgive him, so that your
Father in heaven may forgive you your sins."*

MARK 11:25

If we've asked for God's forgiveness through Jesus' sacrifice,
for our terribly long list of offenses against Him, He's already
forgiven us. Why would we do less for those—including our
spouses—who have wronged us?

Some husbands and wives seem highly invested in keeping
minutes of all past sins and offenses of their spouses. *Ka-ching,
ka-ching, ka-ching*—the cash register of marital history just
keeps adding up the injustices, great and small, perceived and
real.

One day that gunny sack of unforgiven hurts becomes so
heavy that the aggrieved spouse, irritated by some insignifi-
cant infraction, feels the irresistible urge to dump them on the
other's head. The recipient feels righteously indignant that a
major injustice, a massive overreaction to nothing, has been

perpetrated on him or her. This exchange, born of many choices not to forgive, solves nothing, resolves nothing, heals nothing.

Failing to forgive also gets a relationship stuck in an unending, repetitive cycle of blaming each other—rather than taking responsibility for one's shortcomings. This is a terrible model for children to follow and to pass on to future generations.

But what about offenses that seem almost unforgivable? What about a father who sexually abuses his children, or an unrepentant wife who flaunts a lesbian affair? How do you forgive that?

Ultimately, forgiveness is an attitude—one that may be understood only by you and the Lord. It's giving up your insistence on getting revenge. It is not sweeping a crime under the rug or denying the enormity of what an offender has done.

In the case of abuse, your first action may need to be ensuring your safety and that of your children. Forgiving a violent or perverted spouse is not the same as being naïve or stupid about his or her potential to do further harm.

Forgiveness is also not equivalent to forgetting a spouse's track record. It doesn't mean that an abusive husband or wife will be immediately allowed back into the family home after a quick, superficial, even tearful "repentance." It doesn't mean that an unfaithful spouse must be welcomed back without a commitment to counseling and behavior change.

There are times, for example, when a wife is afraid to forgive her serially adulterous husband for fear that he'll only betray and hurt her again. Her instincts may be exactly right; he'll be chasing another skirt within a month. Forgiving him does not mean that she must permit him to continue his sinful lifestyle and remain in a sham marriage to her.

If you're at the edge of this cliff, married to an abusive spouse or a mate who's continued to trash you and your marriage vows through sexual infidelity, seek the help of a pastor or Christian marriage counselor.

If the situation isn't that grave, but you harbor an unforgiving spirit and find it impossible to let go, ask God to give you the power to *want* to forgive. Then commit yourself to doing so.

"But what good will that do?" you might ask.

First, it will restore your fellowship with God that may have been quenched due to this issue in your spiritual life.

Second, it will open the door—at least in relationships that haven't been irretrievably damaged—to the possibility of healing and restoration with your spouse. It may bring greater intimacy than you've had in a long time.

Finally, it can bring freedom from the bonds of resentment, allowing emotional health—perhaps even better physical health. It can build a greater sense of joy and peace to fill that negative space in your life.

—*Phillip J. Swihart*

WORTH THINKING ABOUT

Read Mark 11:25 again. What does genuine forgiveness feel like? If someone has experienced genuine forgiveness from Christ, why might he or she be tempted to withhold that same kind of forgiveness from his or her spouse?

WORTH PRAYING ABOUT

Thank God for His willingness to forgive, and ask His Holy Spirit to give you that same willingness when it comes to your spouse.

WORTH DOING

Make a list of old hurts and grudges you may be holding against your spouse. Be open and honest. Once you've compiled your lists, read them to each other. When you're done, burn the lists as a symbolic gesture of your willingness to forgive.

47

Staying Faithful

*"Marriage should be honored by all, and
the marriage bed kept pure, for God will judge
the adulterer and all the sexually immoral."*

HEBREWS 13:4

Maybe you've noticed that adultery is a huge problem, even in the church. Perhaps you're worried that your marriage might be the next to crumble.

It's no wonder that infidelity is such a threat. Our culture sets us up; television and movies vividly portray sexual desire as an uncontrollable force, unstoppable by moral or spiritual convictions. Dating relationships start younger and younger, with "serial dating" providing a perfect training ground for serial marriage and physical intimacy outside its bonds.

Even our jobs can threaten our marriages. When we're assigned to travel or work long hours with co-workers of the opposite sex, our boundaries—and marriages—can fall.

Not all adultery is physical, of course. Most physical affairs begin as emotional ones. While an infrequent dream about a sexual encounter with someone else is not necessarily something we can control or should feel guilty over, indulging in daydreams about a co-worker is dangerous.

Viewing pornography is another form of infidelity. Though there's no contact with another person, it's as adulterous as physically touching a partner (see Matthew 5:27-28). Virtual affairs are becoming commonplace, too, as people visit Internet chat rooms at home and work.

Believing some dangerous myths about adultery puts us at further risk. Many of us assume unfaithful spouses must have set out to have an affair, and that we would never choose that option ourselves. But most adulterers who are professing Christians never started the process intending to have an affair.

Another misperception is the idea that the husband is usually the unfaithful partner. A moment of reflection will reveal that for every heterosexual man who commits adultery, there's a woman participating, too.

You may wonder whether infidelity always means the end of a marriage. Surprisingly, it doesn't. Most couples don't divorce after adultery. The offended spouse tends to show great emotional stamina after discovering the affair. Sometimes this is due in part to an unhealthy dependency or neediness; but many times there's an ability to forgive that can only be attributed to God's grace.

Another reason many marriages survive adultery is that God is *for* marriage. While His justice demands we honor Him first, rather than enabling an unrepentant adulterer to continue to sin, He wants to give us a way out of the brokenness.

The best time to deal with infidelity, though, is before it happens. There are ways to protect your marriage.

You can start by becoming informed. Rather than fretting, "If we really trusted each other I wouldn't be concerned about this," you can say, "If I value my marriage I will learn how to protect it."

Basic strategies for guarding your relationship include the following.

1. Don't develop deep friendships with people of the opposite sex. Again, most affairs begin at the emotional level.

2. Bring your marital complaints to your spouse rather than confiding in someone else.

3. Be careful with touch. Dropping physical boundaries is never wise.

4. Don't have private e-mail and phone accounts or keep other significant secrets from your spouse.

5. Avoid business travel or late hours alone with co-workers of the opposite sex. Have a third party present when you work together.

In a larger sense, fending off infidelity means working on the sense of closeness you and your mate share. Adultery is a symptom of intimacy disorder. If your spouse strays, that behavior is only the tip of the iceberg. Under the surface there are damaged thoughts, emotions, and a troubled relationship with God that are the real threats to your ship. If you need the help of a therapist to deal with issues like these, don't hesitate to get it.

—*Rob Jackson*

WORTH THINKING ABOUT

Read Hebrews 13:4 again. Why does God place such an emphasis on purity in marriage? Why do many societies place so little emphasis on it?

WORTH PRAYING ABOUT

Ask God to help you see marriage the way He sees it, as something that needs to be nurtured and protected.

WORTH DOING

Rewrite your wedding vows to address some of the specific challenges you face in your marriage right now. For example: "I promise never to go out alone with a co-worker of the opposite gender." Or, "I promise to tell you when I'm feeling suspicious or insecure, instead of letting those feelings build up inside of me."

48

Respecting Your In-laws

"Honor your father and your mother,
so that you may live long in the land the
LORD your God is giving you."

EXODUS 20:12

"What do I owe my in-laws?"

That's an interesting question. Another way to phrase it might be, "As a son-in-law or daughter-in-law, what's required of me? What are my obligations, whether I feel like it or not, in relating to my spouse's parents?"

The first principle that applies here is that, if you're a Christian, you owe your in-laws behavior that's consistently Christian in character—as you do anyone else. This doesn't ignore the reality that if your in-laws are "difficult" people, are controlling and manipulative, are emotionally or mentally dysfunctional, or don't share your faith, this may be a particularly hard challenge. The problem is that they're not just anyone. They're connected to your spouse through genetics, history, and complex psychological dynamics.

If you have disagreements with your in-laws, your spouse may feel caught in the middle between parents and you. You, meanwhile, have obligations to in-laws and spouse—and children, if you have any.

If you feel your in-laws are intruding into your married life, the old saying, "Good fences make good neighbors," may apply. In concert with your mate, set reasonable boundaries; ask that he or she firmly and kindly insist that your in-laws respect these limits.

"Honoring" one's parents does require showing them patience, kindness, gentleness, and respect. This applies to in-laws, too. You may not even like them, but you need to choose to act in a loving manner toward them. For instance, you might choose to adopt their tradition of having an Easter egg hunt, despite the fact that you don't want your kids to think the Easter bunny is real. Enjoying the family event is possible, even if you follow it with a reminder to the children about the real meaning of the holiday.

When you married, you also became part of another family with its own set of expectations. You need to recognize and respect those—within limits.

What are those limits? Here are three things that "honoring" your in-laws does *not* mean:

• It doesn't require that you submerge all your own feelings, desires, preferences, and needs in the service of "doing things their way."

- It doesn't mean you must permit them to disrespect, control, or manipulate you for their own selfish ends.
- It doesn't entail "obeying" all their "parental" requests or requirements—which, in some instances with some in-laws, may get pretty crazy.

For example, if Herb's parents were to insist that Tina and Herb go on every family vacation with them, like it or not, it would be emotionally pathological and ultimately toxic for Herb and Tina's relationship. Sometimes the most honoring response is to diplomatically but firmly say, "No." Letting in-laws split, manipulate, or control you by silently acceding to their nutty, neurotic, inappropriate demands isn't necessarily showing Christian love.

In-law conflicts grow more complicated when a spouse seems to side with his or her parents and against his or her mate. The mate may rightly feel outnumbered or "ganged up on."

This isn't so much an in-law problem as a marital one. If one spouse remains too dependent upon his or her parents, that needs to be addressed in a straightforward way. If one spouse is blaming the in-laws for a disagreement the couple is experiencing, that should be dealt with, too.

If you've become engaged in a quiet (or not so quiet) war with your in-laws—and maybe also with your spouse—about these tangled issues, don't let it erode your marriage further. Do the healthy thing and seek out a Christian therapist.

—Phillip J. Swihart

WORTH THINKING ABOUT

Read Exodus 20:12 again. How do you give or bring honor to someone? What obstacles need to be overcome in order for you to honor your in-laws in the way God intends?

WORTH PRAYING ABOUT

Ask God to work in your heart so that you can establish a relationship with your in-laws that honors Him as much as it does them.

WORTH DOING

Create a memory album with your in-laws. Gather an assortment of photos of them—with and without your spouse—to compile. Show a genuine interest in their history. Ask questions about the people and places in the pictures. Label the photos for posterity. The goal: to bond with your in-laws over family history.

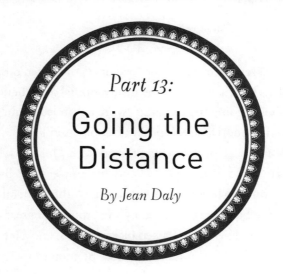

Part 13:

Going the Distance

By Jean Daly

Jim and I love meeting couples who have been married 50, 60, and even 75 years. They always seem to have an enormous smile and a twinkle in their eye when proudly announcing their lifelong accomplishment. It is so sweet. We are always moved by their complete devotion to one another.

It's curious that while the institution of marriage is being challenged, everyone seems to celebrate long-term matrimony. Our society values this commitment so much that the president of the United States, when properly requested to do so, will send a personalized greeting to those couples celebrating 50th, 60th, 70th or later wedding anniversaries. We all enjoy seeing marriages succeed into the twilight.

If you ask us, one of the main reasons divorce is so rampant is because too many people throw in the towel the moment they hit the first serious bump in the road or encounter an obstacle to their plans which appears to be insurmountable. Whenever we think about "going the distance," we're reminded about a story once told by motivational speaker Napoleon Hill.

Mr. Hill was fond of telling the tale of R.U. Darby. During America's Gold Rush, Darby and his uncle were living in Williamsburg, Maryland. When news of the mineral mania reached the East Coast, enticed by the promise of great wealth, Mr. Darby and his uncle packed picks, shovels, and a few necessities, then traveled thousands of miles by train to Colorado.

After several weeks of hard labor digging and shoveling by hand, the men hit pay dirt. With visions of the mother lode dancing in their minds, they carefully concealed their find and returned to Maryland. They needed to raise enough capital to buy the drills and heavy equipment to harvest the gold. The family was quick to pool the cash they needed.

Upon their return to Colorado, they redoubled their efforts and soon discovered their vein of gold was ranked among the richest in Colorado history. All they needed was a few more loads of the precious metal and they'd be able to repay their loans. After that, they'd be living high on the hog.

That's when they were dealt a curve.

The vein ran dry.

How was this possible? Their pot of gold was within reach—they just knew it. For several weeks they drilled and dug. Nothing—just boring, old dirt. Not an ounce of gold was to be found. Discouraged, disillusioned, and still very much in debt, they gave up. They sold the machinery and the rights to the claim to a junk dealer for a few hundred bucks, then went home.

But the story doesn't end there.

The junk dealer was shrewd and immediately sought the advice of a mining engineer experienced in such matters. The engineer studied the dig and returned with startling news: The gold was probably within three feet of where Darby and his uncle had tossed in the towel. Turns out they were uneducated about the behavior of fault lines.

With a smile at this piece of news, the junk man continued the dig. He didn't have far to go—all of three feet! He struck gold. Tons of precious ore were hauled out of what was considered a dead mine. Indeed, it was one of the largest gold finds in Colorado.

It's almost always too soon to quit. If you're still finding your way through the muck and mire of marital woes, we urge you, if at all possible, to keep going. There's a very good chance that you're closer to a breakthrough than you realize.

There's nothing more beautiful than a marriage that goes the distance and stands the test of time. If we want our golden years to shine, we need to spend time every day pouring ourselves into the life of our partner. If we want to be loved, we need to love and serve without ceasing—and we need to do so without regard for what we receive in return.

Does it sound easy? Who said it would be?

Anything beautiful takes time and effort. You can begin with finding some nuggets of truth in the final section that follows.

49

You Don't Have to Drift Apart

"So they are no longer two, but one. Therefore what God has joined together, let man not separate."
MATTHEW 19:6

Robin admits that she and her husband, Tony, are drifting apart. "We have different interests now. He's immersed in his work, and I'm at home all day with our three sons. When Tony gets home, he has nothing left for me. He doesn't really love me."

Many couples seem to feel marriage is like selecting the right plane—and then putting it on autopilot. That's a good way to ensure that spouses eventually drift apart.

Here's how it often works: One partner is satisfied with the relationship as it is, but the other's needs are overlooked. In the case of Robin and Tony, Tony has been the mostly happy one. He has a beautiful wife, three great kids, a relationship with the Lord, and a job he enjoys. He's seen himself as having made the right choices—so from now on, it's smooth sailing. Autopilot has seemed to work for him.

Robin, on the other hand, is wondering whether she made the right choice of "plane." She needs more of Tony's presence to feel valued.

In a bid for Tony's attention, Robin has started distancing herself from him. His reaction is to feel inadequate, disappointed in himself that he can't make his wife happy, unworthy of her love, and confused. He's thinking, *What am I doing wrong?*

Instead of disclosing her needs, Robin is expecting Tony to do some mind reading. When he fails, she withdraws her love. He, in turn, feels rejected and helpless to please her. Closeness evaporates, replaced by confusion and disappointment.

The result: Their relationship feels empty. They're drifting apart.

Robin and Tony need to understand that marriage is a growing, living relationship that needs nurturing. Before nurturing can be accepted, though, both partners have to be willing to take responsibility for their feelings and behaviors.

Using "straight talk" to acknowledge emotions without blaming can lead to resolving conflict. Robin could start the process by saying something like, "Tony, when I've had little adult conversation all day, I really need to talk with you."

Is this statement blaming? No. Is it clear what she needs? Yes. This will prevent defensiveness, contempt, and withdrawal.

Robin also can set the stage for solving the problem by putting the kids on a schedule that allows her "alone time" with Tony. The degree of closeness in a marriage reflects the overall climate in a home, and "climate control" takes spending time together.

Robin needs to know how to handle her resentment, too. When thoughts like *He doesn't really love me* arise, what should she do?

When such a thought strolls into the entryway of her mind, it doesn't belong to her yet; she doesn't have to feel guilty about it. But when she "camps on" this resentful thought instead of analyzing and rejecting it, it takes on a life of its own. She accepts ownership and buys into deception. She allows the thought to keep her from respectfully telling Tony what she's experiencing.

There's hope for Robin and Tony. They're both Christians who take their relationship with God seriously, and have been asking Him what to do about drifting apart. With His leading, they're working on making changes like these:

- becoming better listeners;
- taking responsibility for their actions and feelings;
- avoiding blaming;
- being more affectionate and considerate;
- becoming partners in parenting;
- respecting each other's differences;
- supporting each other in extended family conflicts;
- praying individually and as a couple;
- journaling their feelings individually to their heavenly Father;
- placing a priority on time together;

- submitting to God as their authority;
- being proactive by creating a plan.

There are as many reasons for drifting apart as there are marriages. But the way to prevent that drift begins with a single step: taking yourself off autopilot.

—*Betty Jordan*

WORTH THINKING ABOUT

Read Matthew 19:6 again. Why does God intend for marriage to be permanent? What happens in a relationship where divorce is not an option?

WORTH PRAYING ABOUT

Ask God to help you revive your relationship, and to give you a fresh appreciation for your spouse.

WORTH DOING

Sit down together to create a "battle strategy" for protecting your marriage. Be specific with your ideas. Instead of suggesting something vague like, "spending more time together," block out certain times during the week to take a walk, go on a date, or just do chores together.

50

Is It Ever Too Late for a Marriage?

"Let us not become weary in doing good, for at
the proper time we will reap a harvest if we do
not give up. Therefore, as we have opportunity,
let us do good to all people, especially to those
who belong to the family of believers."

GALATIANS 6:9-10

Is it ever too late for a marriage?

Not if God has His way. Not if He's allowed to be an active part of creating healing and peace in the midst of your marital battles and woundedness. Even if there's only a shred of agreement left between you, it can be done.

The tiniest flickering ray of hope can give off enough light to encourage your first, hesitant step toward loving and respecting each other. True, there can be some last-gasp attempts to vindicate angry motives and behaviors. But faith in God's eagerness to heal can furnish the energy you need to thrust your way past such roadblocks.

If your marriage has reached a painfully crushing state of affairs, how can it be rescued and restored?

Perhaps the most insightful and poignant cry for restoration ever penned came from the heart of David, the Israelite king. It's in Psalm 51, which contains core phrases like these:

- "Have mercy" (vs. 1);
- "For I know my transgressions" (vs. 3);
- "You desire truth" (vs. 6);
- "Let me hear joy and gladness" (vs. 8);
- "Create in me a pure heart" (vs. 10);
- "Grant me a willing spirit" (vs. 12);
- "A broken and contrite heart, O God, you will not despise" (vs. 17).

That kind of attitude goes a long way toward rebuilding a marriage. David's confession also reminds us of three things:

- God's hand is extended to us.
- He wants us to heal.
- He will honor our cooperation and forgive our delinquencies.

Restoring your marriage may depend upon your willingness to forgive and honor one another. Still, if earnest self-examination and your attempts to make amends fall short, it will be sensible to concede that you could use help.

If your marriage is stressed to the point of collapse, dedicated professionals can save you time and frustration as you try to make a giant leap back into each other's trust and favor. The guidance of an experienced marriage "mender"—a Christian counselor—can shorten your journey appreciably.

Make no mistake: It won't be easy. Reconciliation poses a genuine challenge and demands your God-given best to produce results. Far too often when a marriage teeters on the edge of disaster, a late burst of stubbornness and pride takes hold; jaws lock in denying the need for anyone else's services.

So the question becomes, "Will you do as well by your marriage as you would by your watch, your car, or your kitchen sink when it requires time, effort, and money?"

Imagine the rewards of mending your relationship. They can be a powerful push, redirecting your thoughts and efforts toward regaining the satisfactions of your lost marital harmony. Just as love's flame flickers from careless inattention, it can be nurtured back to brightness by the decision to take action.

But what if you're the only partner willing to seek counseling? Should you go anyway?

Yes, yes, yes!

Many marriages have been rescued because one spouse took the initiative toward positive change. Often the partner who stayed home became curious and joined the counseling sessions, leading to a change of heart.

Thousands of couples have discovered the effectiveness of good counseling in rebuilding a marriage—even if they started as skeptics.

—*Sam Kennedy*

WORTH THINKING ABOUT

Read Galatians 6:9-10 again. How could such persistence and singleness of purpose affect your relationship with your spouse? What can you do about the "weariness" that hinders you from doing what's best for your relationship?

WORTH PRAYING ABOUT

Ask God to help you stoke the flames of your relationship and recognize its importance to Him and to you and your spouse.

WORTH DOING

Spend an evening together recalling the first time you saw or met one another and the way your relationship developed from that point. Where were you? What were the circumstances? What were your initial reactions to each other? When did you know there was something special between you? What obstacles or challenges stood in the way of your relationship? How did you resolve them?

51

Getting Wise Counsel

*"Pride only breeds quarrels, but wisdom
is found in those who take advice."*

PROVERBS 13:10

While premarital counseling has gained popularity, there is still prejudice against couples getting help after the wedding. Some churches have counselors on staff, but many Christians still hear, "Just pray about it." Whether voiced or not, the message seems to be that Christians shouldn't need professional counseling unless they are really bad off.

This attitude virtually ensures that people will have bigger problems, because as happens with a sore tooth or raveling thread, early intervention is key to the solution. Every couple has disagreements, and many work through them effectively on their own or with a pastor. But when a pattern of serious conflict starts to emerge, getting help sooner than later can mean big benefits down the road.

Here are five things you need to know about seeing a marriage counselor.

1. *It's not weird.* And it's not like TV.

Many people avoid going to therapy because they fear they'll have to lie on a couch and reveal secrets to someone who just nods a lot. They may also be afraid they'll have tearful and embarrassing "breakthroughs."

Others avoid the counselor's office because they believe it's too expensive or that it will take years to gain any benefit. But most therapy is actually brief—and, when compared to alternatives like depression, divorce, or chronic anxiety, quite cost-effective. For those who need it, counseling is not so much an expense as it is an investment.

Professional counseling is a relationship with safety built in. Professional ethics ensure you will be treated with respect and care. Conversations that occur in the counselor's office could happen as easily at home. The purpose is to affirm, not tear down, and the main task is equipping. As you talk, the counselor tailors his or her professional knowledge to your personal situation.

2. *Christians need Christian therapy.* When looking for the right counselor, a good starting place is your local church. Ask for referral to a counselor who's licensed and uses a Christ-centered, biblically sound approach.

3. *Be prepared to deal with the whole picture.* Most of us tend to get preoccupied with one or two pieces of our lives. Even therapists run this risk, as they offer communication training to those who actually communicate very well with everyone but their spouse or children.

Often the "big picture" includes the influence of your family of origin. It makes no more sense to ignore that influence on your current conflicts than it would to polish the leaves on a tree suffering from root damage. A good counselor will help you look at your marital issues in context, exploring family systems as well as integrating your relationship with Christ.

4. *It's worth the sacrifice.* At first, the decision to seek counsel may seem to make your life more complicated. Identifying a good therapist, rearranging your budget, securing child care if needed, and negotiating with a spouse may make sweeping your issues under the rug look appealing. But the longer you put off dealing with the real problems, the more complex they become.

5. *Deep wounds need deep treatment.* Some issues, such as abortion, addiction, or sexuality, have deep spiritual ramifications. These topics can cause shame and fear to well up dramatically and unexpectedly. They deserve the intensive care of a professional counselor trained to deal with them.

—*Rob Jackson*

WORTH THINKING ABOUT

Read Proverbs 13:10 again. How can you tell if pride is having a negative impact on your relationship? How could someone earn your trust as an advisor?

WORTH PRAYING ABOUT

Ask God to bring people into your lives who can advise you in your relationship, and ask Him for the wisdom to recognize good advice and the humility to follow it.

WORTH DOING

Spend some time talking about the best and worst advice you ever received. Recall people who surprised you with their wisdom and the ones who didn't know what they were talking about. Discuss the benefits you enjoyed from following good advice and the mistakes you made while following bad advice. Consider how your past experiences color your attitude toward marital counseling.

52

What Makes a Marriage Last?

*"Above all, love each other deeply, because
love covers over a multitude of sins."*

1 PETER 4:8

Many psychologists believe the greatest predictor of a lasting marriage is a commitment to marriage itself.

A sense of humor on the part of both spouses doesn't hurt, either.

Of course, just knowing this won't necessarily make your marriage last longer. But the right attitude *will* help ensure that your partnership is a lifelong one.

To maintain that attitude, remember that this experience called marriage is a relationship. It's not a possession. Yes, we do say "*my* wife" or "*my* husband," but that simply sets boundaries for others outside your marriage to recognize and respect. It's all yours—to protect and nourish.

How are you supposed to apply these principles in everyday life? Try the following tips.

1. *Go beyond words.* Smiles and hugs help your spouse know the "I love yous" are genuine. Something about the warmth of a caring embrace generates a sense of acceptance and worth.

2. *Lower your weapons.* Emotional traffic flows more smoothly when you honor the "Yield" signs. Remember that no one is everlastingly right.

3. *Don't get smug.* Deny yourself the sour satisfaction of gloating. Without fail it creates festering resentment.

4. *Drop the barbs.* Cleverness slides all too easily into the hurtfulness of sarcasm, which can be deadly to a healthy marriage.

Speaking of communication, that's an area that deserves special attention. Often counselors hear clients complain, "We just can't communicate!" Actually, that isn't precisely the case. We're all communicators; we can't *not* communicate!

We can be selective, even negative, in the messages we send—but send them we will. As lifelong communicators, you can take inventory of the messages you're sending and select the ones which bring happy results. While you're at it, you can demonstrate a bit of wisdom by discarding the unproductive ones.

Give each other the benefit of the doubt as you proceed with caution and tact. Low-key suggestions are usually most helpful. Directness is okay, but sidestep bluntness. And avoid communication styles like the following.

1. *Accuse and blame.* This is an attempt to shift responsibility and a refusal to accept accountability. It's infuriating. A common scenario goes something like this: "Well, if you were the spouse I need you to be, then I wouldn't have to look somewhere else."

2. *Inanity.* This avoids the subject and leaves your mate frustrated. Take a typical instance: Doug's exasperated over a flat tire when it's time to leave for work; Vanessa chirps, "Don't the tires on the Browns' new SUV look great?"

3. *I did this for you.* This employs witty but phony justification for actions that are self-serving or uncaring. The bills aren't paid, but Wayne shows up with a snappy sports car and says to his wife, "This red goes just great with your hair!"

4. *The lockout.* He—and it is more often the husband—either storms from the scene or uses stony silence as punishment and refusal to allow access to himself. Thus he defeats any realistic hope of settling differences.

5. *How could you?* Outraged innocence and supersensitive righteousness are used to shut down any chance of movement toward resolving issues. The supposed victim's voice might quaver as she wipes away a tear: "How on earth could you ever say such a thing?"

None of this is all that complicated. But husbands and wives who've made a journey of many years together know that theirs is a marriage of more than convenience; it's a commitment. Divorce was never considered an option.

Welcome to the world of the fulfilling partnership called marriage. Your wedding vows will remain bright and buoyant as you understand your goals and relish pursuing them together.

—*Sam Kennedy*

WORTH THINKING ABOUT

Read 1 Peter 4:8 again. What personal shortcomings and mistakes does your spouse's love for you cover over? How can you show your thankfulness to your spouse for loving you so deeply?

WORTH PRAYING ABOUT

Thank God for His role in giving your marriage strength and endurance, and ask Him to help you deepen your love for your spouse.

WORTH DOING

Start a new hobby or other activity together—one neither of you has done before. You might try a baking class, scuba diving, ice skating, or anything else that appeals to both of you. Let your shared inexperience bring you closer together.

EPILOGUE

By Jim and Jean

One of our favorite movies is *The Princess Bride*. At one point in this playful story, Westley (a.k.a. "Farm boy" and the "Dread Pirate Robert") looks the lovely Princess Buttercup in the eye and offers this sobering bit of insight: "Life is pain, Highness. Anyone who says differently is selling something."

Westley was right. Life on this side of the Garden of Eden is filled with pain, and the pain is especially acute when it manifests itself in a bad marriage. Anybody dealing with a challenging relationship sees this. We all know Westley hit the nail on the head with his observation.

The larger question, though, is how we respond to the discomfort when it comes our way. Will we be crushed by it? Or will we get whatever help we need to overcome the struggle, the conflict, or the circumstances?

Addressing the source of the problem means confronting it straight on—a technique that can be very difficult but effective if handled deftly. If it was pain that prompted you to read this book, we hope you'll let us know how you and your spouse responded to the ideas and advice. If you need more help, don't hesitate to call Focus on the Family. Our licensed Christian counselors are available to take your call at 1-855-771-HELP (1-855-771-4357).

If you'd like to get in touch with a counselor in your area, Focus on the Family also maintains a referral network of Christian therapists. For information, just call the Counseling Department at the number above.

Marriage is God's idea; because He invented it, we shouldn't be surprised that according to recently released census data, the quickest way to happiness is also the oldest way:

Get and stay married.

According to the Heritage Foundation, intact families generally do better financially; on average, single men's income is only 60 percent of married men's, with single women earning just 40 percent of what wives make. Marriage can make child poverty at least 80 percent less likely. And that's without mentioning the apparent boost that marriage gives to physical and emotional health.[4] And despite the chronic plague of divorce in America, the U.S. Census recently found that for couples wed after 1990, marriages are lasting longer.[5]

So, as Mark Twain once said of the music of Richard Wagner, "It's not nearly as bad as it sounds."

This good news doesn't help soothe the pain or heal the hurt of the couple who, this very day, has decided to throw in the towel. Divorce remains a major problem in our culture—and among Christians.

If we were to sum up the essence of Christian marriage in a single word, what would it be?

We might suggest the word "other"—because in order for

a marriage to thrive, each spouse must be sacrificial and selfless towards the other. Marriage is really not about your happiness, but about you helping your spouse become the person God made him or her to be.

It's just a bonus that a healthy marriage will increase your happiness and satisfaction, too!

In the end, perhaps Benjamin Franklin didn't quite have it right when he said that the key to health, wealth, and wisdom was to get to bed early and rise at dawn. Instead, if you want all those things and more, feel free to sleep in tomorrow. Just make sure it's with your spouse with whom you'll spend the rest of your life.

We hope you've enjoyed your journey through this book. From this point on, the very best thing you can do for your spouse and your marriage is to fall more deeply in love with Jesus.

C.S. Lewis once pondered the question of whether it's possible to love another too much. Here's his conclusion:

> We may love another person too much in proportion
> to our love for God. But it is the smallness of our love
> for God, not the greatness of our love for the man that
> constitutes the inordinacy.[6]

In other words, it's not about loving your spouse less. It's about loving your Lord more. Best wishes as you take that road together.

NOTES

1. http://www.cbsnews.com/8301-18560_162-621356 .html.
2. Erich Fromm, *The Art of Loving* (Harper Perennial Modern Classics, 2006), p. 52.
3. Bill and Pam Farrel, *Red-Hot Monogamy* (Harvest House, 2006), p. 9.
4. http://familyfacts.org/briefs/marriage-and-family.
5. http://abcnews.com/US/long-lasting-marriages-rise-US -census-report/story?id=13638606#.UZPpfq4mcZc.
6. C.S. Lewis, *The Four Loves* (Mariner Books, 1971), p. 122.

FOCUS ON THE FAMILY®

Welcome to the Family

Whether you purchased this book, borrowed it, or received it as a gift, thanks for reading it! This is just one of many insightful, biblically based resources that Focus on the Family produces for people in all stages of life.

Focus is a global Christian ministry dedicated to helping families thrive as they celebrate and cultivate God's design for marriage and experience the adventure of parenthood. Our outreach exists to support individuals and families in the joys and challenges they face, and to equip and empower them to be the best they can be.

Through our many media outlets, we offer help and hope, promote moral values and share the life-changing message of Jesus Christ with people around the world.

Focus on the Family MAGAZINES

These faith-building, character-developing publications address the interests, issues, concerns, and challenges faced by every member of your family from preschool through the senior years.

For More INFORMATION

 ONLINE:
Log on to
FocusOnTheFamily.com
In Canada, log on to
FocusOnTheFamily.ca

 PHONE:
Call toll-free:
800-A-FAMILY
(232-6459)
In Canada, call toll-free:
800-661-9800

THRIVING FAMILY®
Marriage & Parenting

FOCUS ON THE FAMILY CLUBHOUSE JR.®
Ages 4 to 8

FOCUS ON THE FAMILY CLUBHOUSE®
Ages 8 to 12

FOCUS ON THE FAMILY CITIZEN®
U.S. news issues

Rev. 3/11

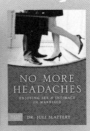